CRIMINAL SENTENCES

CRIMINAL SENTENCES

Law without Order

by Marvin E. Frankel

HILL AND WANG NEW YORK

A division of Farrar, Straus and Giroux

First printing, 1973
Library of Congress catalog card number: 72-95111
ISBN: 0-8090-3709-2
Published simultaneously in Canada
by Doubleday Canada Ltd., Toronto
Printed in the United States of America
4 5 6 7 8 9 0

For Alice, Eleanor, David, Ellen, and Mara

Preface

The central purpose of this small volume is to seek the attention of literate citizens—not primarily lawyers and judges, but not excluding them—for gross evils and defaults in what is probably the most critical point in our system of administering criminal justice, the imposition of sentence.

The sentence is critical for obvious reasons. For one thing, the great majority (ranging in some jurisdictions to around 90 percent) of those formally charged with crimes plead guilty. So it is a matter of the first importance, and tragically incongruous, that we weave the most elaborate procedures to safeguard the rights of those who stand trial, but then treat as a casual anticlimax the perfunctory process of deciding whether, and for how long, the defendant will be locked away or otherwise "treated." This is not, obviously, to urge removal of the trial protections—though there are those among us (not I) who see that as a vital objective. It is simply to say that the neglect by all of us of sentencing should no longer be tolerated.

The sentence is also critical because it is (or should be) the fundamental judgment determining how, where, and why the offender should be dealt with for what may be much or all of his remaining life. There has been much professed concern lately over the horrors of American prisons and the flaws generally in correctional practices. Nothing I have to say should be supposed to deprecate that concern. Indeed, as will appear, it is not possible to consider the grave defects in our sentencing practices without dealing at least a little with the interrelated subjects of prison and parole. But the fact remains that the prison is situated along a course charted initially at the stage of sentencing. Whatever his other faults, the jailer is scarcely to be blamed if the judgment he is assigned to administer has been imposed without any clear sense of purpose. If the sentence is for "punishment," how agreeable should the dungeon be? If the sentence is for "rehabilitation," is it acceptable to use the same prison as the one serving to punish? If we mean both to punish and to rehabilitate, is such a thing possible? Simple questions like these are basic and seemingly inescapable. It is remarkable, then, how completely we have managed to escape them while imposing millions of years of imprisonment—to say nothing of the legalized killings—over the last century or two.

This book, to state its *raison d'être* in a word or two, is submitted to urge that questions like those just stated be evaded no longer. The main thing is to begin to confront the problems. Beyond that, tentatively and with diffidence, I propose to suggest possible directions of work toward improvements, if not "solutions."

What I have to say is prompted, of course, by the daily work with which I have been privileged, and burdened, since November 1965.* This is not meant, however, as a "con-

* Thus prompted, the discussion will tend to have the federal felony sentence as the concrete model in view. Differences, and a number of specialized problems, would be found in other contexts—for a notable example, in so-called petty state courts where huge numbers of people have first and frequent tastes of the criminal law. Nevertheless, the basic issues I mean to raise pervade the field.

fession," though I do refer inevitably to personal experiences and observations both to illustrate points and to account for my views. This is not an "exposé," either, though some of the publicly knowable facts have shocked me when I have confronted them. However fashionable it may be to serve up the inside dope, I cannot fairly pretend to be doing that. The evils I mean to portray are grim. They have come to impress me as unbearable by any society that styles itself civilized. But they are not secret or mysterious. Nor are they assignable to any handy set of villains. While there is ample blame to share among the judges, lawyers, legislators, and all of us, the fundamental problem, as usual, is in the system, or lack of it.

The heart of the matter, as I see it, is that we have chosen, or permitted ourselves, to stop thinking about the criminal process after the drama of apprehension, trial, and conviction (or plea) has ended. "Convicts" are outlaws to us. Their plight is dreary and "deserved." Preferring lovely or exciting things, we draw curtains over such dank subjects. We have managed, until lately at least, to warehouse our offenders in faraway dungeons, away from their families as well as the rest of us, and to forget them. We have shuffled them off by sentencing judgments pronounced speedily and with relative ease, despite all the protestations of agony on the part of the sentencing judges.

This easy course is becoming daily less viable. In the roiling of our world, we are being compelled to reckon with the explosive pressures of those who were until just the other day voiceless and without rights. It has become easy and accepted to heed such pressures from "respectable" quarters—those we now acknowledge as human despite their poverty or pigmentation. It may be less easy, but it is not much less necessary, to attend to the more disreputable of our fellow beings, including those who mount riots in our prisons.

While the expectation of nobility and virtue is not the

most solid foundation for planning human affairs, I would hope that our need to humanize criminal sentencing will be served for reasons more worthy than the fear of disaster. It is to be hoped at a minimum that most of us will recognize how we are all demeaned when we proceed in the name of the law to be arbitrary, cruel, and lawless. It is with this species of restrained hope that I submit the following observations and proposals.*

* The bulk of these thoughts was tendered, in somewhat more condensed and technical form, as the 1971 Marx Lectures at the University of Cincinnati Law School, published in the April 1972 issue of that school's Law Review.

Contents

Part One

THE PROBLEM

I

Law without Order or Limit

WE BOAST that ours is a "government of laws, not of men." We do not mean by the quoted principle that men make no difference in the administration of law. Among the basic things we do mean is that all of us, governors and governed alike, are or ought to be bound by laws of general and equal application. We mean, too, that in a just legal order, the laws should be knowable and intelligible so that, to the fullest extent possible, a person meaning to obey the law may know his obligations and predict within decent limits the legal consequences of his conduct.

The broad principle applies with special point to the criminal law, where one of its expressions is in the hoary solemnity of an ancient Latin canon, *Nullum crimen, nulla poena, sine lege*—meaning there can be no crime, *and no punishment,* except as a law prescribes it. Again, the premise embodies the idea of a law reasonably precise and specific. The point was made with characteristic vigor by Mr. Justice Hugo L. Black. Though the quoted words were written in the course of a dissent, they are not matters for debate among us:

> Experience, and wisdom flowing out of that experience, long ago led to the belief that agents of government should not be vested with power and discretion to define and punish as criminal past conduct which had not been clearly defined as a crime in advance. To this end, at least in part, written laws came into being, marking the boundaries of conduct for which public agents could thereafter impose punishment upon people. In contrast, bad governments either wrote no general rules of conduct at all, leaving that highly important task to the unbridled discretion of government agents at the moment of trial, or sometimes, history tells us, wrote their laws in an unknown tongue so that people could not understand them or else placed their written laws at such inaccessible spots that people could not read them.*

The agreed principles the Justice invoked would not be served, obviously, by a "law" proclaiming that "Anything deemed wrong by the Supreme Potentate (or a judge or a jury or anyone) shall be suitably punishable by imprisonment or death." If that quoted hypothetical seems too absurdly extreme to notice, or if the Latin aphorism sounds too utterly trite, it may pay to recall now and then how much blood and sacrifice have been spent for the seeming banality. It is worth remembering that through much of recorded history, men have lived under the tyranny of "laws" scarcely less arbitrary and unpredictable than my imaginary provision for the unfettered will of the Supreme Potentate. And before the reference to "history" leads to an excess of contemporary smugness, let me hasten to the present point of this discussion: that the principle of *nulla poena sine lege* is largely ignored by the penalty provisions of our criminal laws.

Our system does tolerably well in following part of the Latin maxim—the part that says *nullum crimen* (no crime) except under law. With some exceptions—not necessarily insignificant ones, but still fairly called exceptions—we follow the precept that conduct may not be branded criminal unless

* *Ginzburg* v. *United States*. 383 U.S. 463, 477 (1966).

it has been proscribed by a reasonably intelligible law in advance of its occurrence. We strive, with a decent measure of success, to follow this famous pronouncement of our Supreme Court in a decision of early 1926: "a statute which either forbids or requires the doing of an act in terms so vague that men of common intelligence must necessarily guess at its meaning and differ as to its application, violates the first essential of due process of law." * But while that standard is generally implemented with respect to the laws' definitions of crimes, it is generally ignored in the portions of the same laws prescribing the range of permissible punishments. As to the penalty that may be imposed, our laws characteristically leave to the sentencing judge a range of choice that should be unthinkable in a "government of laws, not of men."

To underscore it by repetition, my first basic point is this: the almost wholly unchecked and sweeping powers we give to judges in the fashioning of sentences are terrifying and intolerable for a society that professes devotion to the rule of law.

For examples of such unbounded "discretion" (as it is called), it might suffice to consult the common experience of almost anyone even slightly acquainted with the criminal law. Let me recall only a few from the federal criminal code, with which I work. An assault upon a federal officer may be punishable by a fine and imprisonment for "not more than" ten years. The federal kidnapping law authorizes "imprisonment for any term of years or for life." Rape, which (believe it or not) may be a federal offense, leads to "death, or imprisonment for any term of years or for life." ** To take some of our most common federal crimes—driving a stolen

* *Connally* v. *General Construction Co.*, 269 U.S. 385, 391 (1926).

** "Whoever, within the special maritime and territorial jurisdiction of the United States [ships, federal land, buildings, etc.], commits rape shall suffer death, or imprisonment for any term of years or for life." U.S. Code, Title 18, section 2031.

car across state lines may result in a term of "not more than five years," robbing a federally insured bank "not more than twenty-five years," and a postal employee's theft of a letter "not more than five years." The key phrase is, of course, the "not more than." It proclaims that federal trial judges, answerable only to their varieties of consciences, may and do send people to prison for terms that may vary in any given case from none at all up to five, ten, thirty, or more years. This means in the great majority of federal criminal cases that a defendant who comes up for sentencing has no way of knowing or reliably predicting whether he will walk out of the courtroom on probation, or be locked up for a term of years that may consume the rest of his life, or something in between.

I would not wish to exaggerate; the reality is horrid enough without that. Defendants and their lawyers are able to anticipate within broad ranges in a fair number of cases. It is unlikely that the convicted murderer will be freed on the spot—though he may be. There are cases (depending upon the judge) in which probation is a good bet, though not a sure thing. But the law as it is written, and as it operates upon hapless defendants, is not significantly more knowable or predictable than the unregulated sentencing provisions indicate on their face. It is even an illicit form of qualification to insert a parenthetical "depending upon the judge," as I did a couple of sentences ago. For that goes, after all, to the very core of the evil our principles denounce. We claim, remember, to have a government of laws, not men. That promise to the ear is broken to the hope * when a sentence may range from zero up to thirty or more years in the unfettered discretion of miscellaneous judges.

* "And be these juggling fiends no more believ'd,
That palter with us in a double sense;
That keep the word of promise to our ear,
And break it to our hope." *Macbeth*, v. 7. 48–51.

The result, to be dwelt upon a little in the next chapter, is a wild array of sentencing judgments without any semblance of the consistency demanded by the ideal of equal justice. And it could not be otherwise under our non-system of so-called laws prescribing penalties.

The broad statutory ranges might approach a degree of ordered rationality if there were prescribed any standards for locating a particular case within any range. But neither our federal law nor that of any state I know contains meaningful criteria for this purpose. Our Congress and state legislatures have failed even to study and resolve the most basic of the questions affecting criminal penalties, the questions of justification and purpose. Why do we impose punishment? Or is it properly to be named "punishment"? Is our purpose retributive? Is it to deter the defendant himself or others in the community from committing crimes? Is it for reform? rehabilitation? incapacitation of dangerous people? Questions like these have engaged philosophers and students of the criminal law for centuries. There are no easy—probably no single, simple—answers. But perhaps differing from concerns about angels and pins, these problems as to the purposes of criminal sanctions are, or should be, at the bedrock of any rational structure of criminal law. It makes all the difference in the world, for instance, whether we think, as it is fashionable nowadays to say, that only rehabilitation of the offender can justify confinement. It is impossible on that premise to order a week in jail for the elderly official finally caught after years of graft, now turned out of office and disgraced, and neither in need of nor susceptible to any extant kinds of rehabilitation. Leaving this subject for the time being (see Chapter 9), I make the point that our legislators have not done the most rudimentary job of enacting meaningful sentencing "laws" when they have neglected even to sketch democratically determined statements of basic purpose. Left at large, wandering in deserts of uncharted discretion, the judges suit their own value systems insofar as they think about the problem at all.

It may be supposed by many that the broad discretion of the sentencing judge is actually limited by the discipline of the profession, including a body of criteria for placing a given case within the statutory range of up to "not more than" life in prison. The supposition would, unfortunately, be without substantial basis. There are, to be sure, some vague species of curbstone notions—gravity of the particular offense, defendant's prior record, age, background, etc.—that are thought to serve as guides in the particular case. But there is no agreement at all among the sentencers as to what the relevant criteria are or what their relative importance may be. Again, the point is made in all its stark horror by the compelling evidence that widely unequal sentences are imposed every day in great numbers for crimes and criminals not essentially distinguishable from each other.

The sentencing powers of the judges are, in short, so far unconfined that, except for frequently monstrous maximum limits, they are effectively subject to no law at all. Everyone with the least training in law would be prompt to denounce a statute that merely said the penalty for crimes "shall be any term the judge sees fit to impose." A regime of such arbitrary fiat would be intolerable in a supposedly free society, to say nothing of being invalid under our due-process clause. But the fact is that we have accepted unthinkingly a criminal code creating in effect precisely that degree of unbridled power.

Beyond their failure to impose meaningful limits upon the judges, our criminal codes have displayed bizarre qualities of illogic and incongruity. Studies in the recent past revealed such things as these: a Colorado statute providing a ten-year maximum for stealing a dog, while another Colorado statute prescribed six months and a $500 fine for killing a dog; in Iowa, burning an empty building could lead to as much as a twenty-year sentence, but burning a church or school carried a maximum of ten; breaking into a car to steal from its glove compartment could result in up to fifteen years in California, while stealing the entire car carried a maximum of ten. Examples like these could be multiplied. The specific ones I cite may have been repaired in recent revisions. Their essentially illustrative character remains a fair reflection of the haphazard, disorderly qualities of our criminal penalty provisions. And while this motley look is disturbing, it is, of course, less fundamentally atrocious than the characteristic allowance of unfettered discretion to the sentencing judge selecting a term anywhere up to the high maximum.

Both qualities—the crazy-quilt statutory patterns and the blank-check powers of judges—reflect a number of important, if not uniformly pleasant, things about our society. In one of his many quotable insights—though it was not by any means exclusively his—Winston Churchill said:

> The mood and temper of the public with regard to the treatment of crime and criminals is one of the most unfailing tests of the civilization of any country.

The "mood and temper" reflected in our laws assigning punishments include a kind of simpleminded puritanism in which it is premised that conduct we dislike will end or sharply decrease if we pass a criminal law, with harsh sanctions, against it. Many of our criminal laws are enacted in an access of righteous indignation, with legislators fervidly outshouting each other, with little thought or attention given to the large numbers of years inserted as maximum penalties. Written at the random, accidental times when particular evils come to be perceived, the statutes are not harmonized or coordinated with each other. The resulting jumbles of harsh anomalies are practically inevitable.

The more profound problem of excessive judicial power reflects a congeries of causes, advertent and accidental. To look only at the most important and positive of these, the prevalent thesis of the last hundred years or so has been that the treatment of criminals must be "individualized." The Mikado's boast, we have proudly thought, was silly; the punishment in a civilized society must fit the unique criminal, not the crime. The "crime," after all, may describe with a single, mechanical label kinds of misconduct and, more importantly, kinds of individual offenders displaying no similarities of any substantial sort. To assign rigidly a prescribed penalty for each crime (the so-called "tariff" system) is Procrustean. Sentiments like these carried the day long ago; it is scarcely imaginable that they could be questioned today.

Yet it is high time to question and confine them. Like all good ideas allowed to bloom without pruning or other attention, the notion of individualized sentencing has gotten quite out of hand. Reverting to elementary principles for a bit, we ought to recall that individualized justice is prima facie at war with such concepts, at least as fundamental, as equality, objectivity, and consistency in the law. It is not self-evident that the flesh-and-blood judge coming (say) from among the white middle classes will inevitably achieve admirable results when he individualizes the narcotics sentences of the suburban college youth and the street-wise young ghetto hustler. More importantly and more generally, is it perfectly clear that we want our judges to have such power? In most matters of the civil law, while our success is variable, the quest is steadily for certainty, predictability, objectivity. The businessman wants to know what the tax will be on the deal, what the possible "exposure" may be from one risk or another. His lawyer may predict more or less successfully. But what no businessman wants (if he is honest) is a system of "individualized" taxes and exposures, depending upon who the judge or other official may turn out to be and how that decision-maker may assess the case and the individual before him.

This does not mean, of course, that everybody pays the same tax or is held to the same standards of liability. It does mean that the variations are made to turn upon objective, and objectively ascertainable, criteria—impersonal in the sense of the maxim that the law "is no respecter of persons"—and, above all, not left for determination in the wide-open, uncharted, standardless discretion of the judge administering "individualized" justice. The law's detachment is thought to be one of our triumphs. There is dignity and security in the assurance that each of us—plain or beautiful, rich or poor, black, white, tall, curly, whatever—is promised treatment as a bland, fungible "equal" before the law.

Is "individualized" sentencing consistent with that promise? Certainly not under the broad grants of subjective discretion we give to our judges under most American criminal codes today. The ideal of individualized justice is by no means an unmitigated evil, but it must be an ideal of justice *according to law*. This means we must reject individual distinctions—discriminations, that is—unless they can be justified by relevant tests capable of formulation and application with sufficient objectivity to ensure that the results will be more than the idiosyncratic ukases of particular officials, judges or others. I think an approach to such a standard is possible. I shall attempt to sketch it later on. In the meantime, however, if we had to choose between our status quo and a system of narrow "tariffs" for each category of crime, only my prejudiced belief that many judges are humane would make me pause in preferring the latter.

Having said that, let me flee from the appearance of undue complacency about the judges. The judges simply are not good enough—nobody could be—to redress the fundamental absurdities of the system. Some thoughts about the character and limits of the sentencers are the business of the next chapter.

2

Individualized Judges

THE ABSURDITIES of our sentencing laws would remain aesthetically repulsive, but might be otherwise tolerable, if our judges were uniformly brilliant, sensitive, and humane. Though I yield only to numerous judges in my admiration for those on the bench, I must acknowledge that we do not, in fact, approach any such state of affairs. Judges, I think, tend to be like people, perhaps even some cuts above the mine run but, unfortunately, less than gods or angels. And how, after all, could we dream it might be otherwise? Consider whence we acquire our judges, how we select them, how they are trained before and after they don robes.

To start near the beginning, most of our judges have been trained as lawyers. (There is a disappearing breed of petty magistrates for whom this is not necessarily true, and the picture is more bleak with respect to them.) Substantially nothing in the law curriculum is relevant to problems of sentencing. Indeed, until the last decade or so, the entire field of criminal law, being neither lucrative nor prestigious, occupied only a small and disfavored corner of our law schools' attention. While that state of neglect has undergone extensive repairs, these have scarcely grazed the area of interest here. Law students learn something about the rules of the criminal law, about the trial of cases, and, increasingly, about the rights of defendants before and during trial. They receive almost no instruction pertinent to sentencing. They may hear some fleeting references to the purposes of criminal penalties—some generalities about retribution, deterrence, etc. But so far as any intentional consequences of their legal education are concerned, they are taught by people and exposed to curricula barren of even food for thought about sentencing.*

From among the total supply of law graduates who have not studied sentencing, there emerges in twenty or thirty years the narrower group from which we select the bulk of our judges. The most notable thing about this group for present purposes is that its members have mostly remained unencumbered by any exposure to, or learning about, the problems of sentencing. Characterized by their dominant attributes, our judges are men (mostly) of no longer tender years who have not associated much with criminal defendants, who have not seemed shrilly unorthodox, who have not lived recently in poverty, who have been modestly or more successful in their profession. They are likely to have had more than an average lawyer's amount of experience in the courtroom, though it is a little remarkable how large a

* Everything in law, as in life, has exceptions. So I should acknowledge that there are here and there in the law schools some meaningful offerings on the subject. Professor Leonard Orland of the University of Connecticut Law School has lately been giving a well-stocked course on post-conviction matters, including significant and provocative ideas about sentencing. My thoughtful and energetic colleague on the Federal District Court for the Southern District of New York, Judge Harold R. Tyler, Jr., has been finding time in recent years to offer enlightenment on similar subjects at the New York University School of Law. I am certain there are other things of the sort in progress elsewhere. The general point I have made remains basically accurate even today and was sound without noticeable qualification when people now judging went to law school.

percentage of those who go on the bench lack this credential.* They are unlikely to have defended more than a couple of criminal cases, if that many. They are more likely to have done a stint as prosecutors, usually as a brief chapter in the years shortly after law school. However much or little they have been exposed to the criminal trial process, most people ascending (as we say) the bench have paid only the most fleeting and superficial attention to matters affecting the sentences of convicted defendants. In this respect, the pattern set in the law school is carried forward and reenforced. The professional show ends with the verdict or the plea. The histrionics later on at the sentencing proceeding may be moving or embarrassing, even effective on occasion, but are no part of the skills the average lawyer prizes and polishes as special tools of his trade.

Whatever few things may be said for them, our procedures for selecting judges do not improve the prospects of sensitive, knowledgeable sentencing. It may happen sometimes, but I do not recall ever hearing anything relevant to that subject in discussions of the qualifications of prospective judges. I put to one side for this purpose the disgraceful process, widely used, of political nominations, where the candidates are too often selected without concern for any of the qualities supposedly wanted in suitable judges. Even where relevant questions are asked, the professional criteria, reflecting the training and the profession at work, simply do not include meaningful inquiries as to whether the prospective

* I am not myself in a position for exuberant stone-throwing. Before I became a trial judge in 1965, I had spent many years working mainly as an appellate lawyer. I had tried some cases and done a fair amount of trial lawyer's work, but had managed somehow never to face a jury. I had argued criminal appeals, but had never been on either side of a criminal trial. In defense of myself and the bar-association committees that found me acceptable, if not the answer to their prayers, I think it fair to add that the mechanics and economics of big-city law practice lead the members of large, respectable law firms to settle most of their clients' disputes short of actual trial.

judge is fit to wield the awesome sentencing power. Apart from elementary, and usually superficial, glances at vague qualities of "temperament," we would not know really where to look or what to ask on a subject destined to loom so large among the prospective judge's impacts upon his fellow citizens.

The judges fetched up in the process are a mixed bag, without many surprises. Some grow to be concerned and spend substantial time brooding about their sentencing responsibilities. Most, I think, are not so preoccupied. Judges are commonly heard to say that sentencing is the grimmest and most solemnly absorbing of their tasks. This is not exactly hypocrisy. It is, however, among the less meaningful things judges report about their work. Measured by the time devoted to it, by the amount of deliberation and study before each decision, and by the attention to the subject as a field of intellectual concern in general, the judges' effective expenditures of themselves in worries over sentencing do not reflect a profound sense of mission. Judges don't talk much, to each other or to anyone, about the issues and difficulties in sentencing. They don't read or write about such things. Because strictly "legal" problems are rare in this area, and appeals are normally not allowed to attack the sentence (see Chapter 7), the reading pile rarely contains anything pertinent. The judge is likely to read thick briefs, hear oral argument, and then take days or weeks to decide who breached a contract for delivery of onions. The same judge will read a presentence report, perhaps talk to a probation officer, hear a few minutes of pleas for mercy—invest, in sum, less than an hour in all—before imposing a sentence of ten years in prison.

Some judges, confronting the enormities of what they do and how they do it, are visited with occasional onsets of horror or, at least, self-doubt. Learned Hand—to some, the greatest of our judges; to all, among a small handful of the greatest—reflected such sentiments. Never accounted soft toward criminals among any who knew his work, he said of his role in sentencing: "Here I am an old man in a long nightgown making muffled noises at people who may be no worse than I am." A distinguished committee of federal judges, with Hand among its members, acknowledged "the incompetency of certain types of judges to impose sentence." It spoke of judges "not temperamentally equipped" to learn this task acceptably, of judges who compensate for their own inadequacies by "the practice of imposing severe sentences," of judges "who crusade against certain crimes which they feel disposed to stamp out by drastic sentences." * Other judges have expressed similar misgivings—about their own and (perhaps more strongly) about their colleagues' handling of powers so huge and so undefined over the lives of their fellow men.

Self-criticism, uncertainty, and a resultant disposition toward restraint are useful qualities in judges—for sentencing and for other aspects of the job. They are not, however, in oversupply. The kinds of people who make their way onto the bench are not by and large given to humility. If there are seeds of meekness to begin with, the trial bench is not the most fertile place for their cultivation. The trial judge may be reversed with regularity; he may be the butt of lawyers' jokes and an object lesson in the law schools; but the incidents of his daily life—the rituals of deference, the high bench, the visible evidences of power asserted directly and face-to-face—are not designed to shrink his self-image. It should be said in all fairness that the Hamlets of this world are not suited to the business of presiding over trial courts. Scores of things must be decided every day. It is often more important, as Brandeis taught, that the decisions be made than that they be correct. Both the volume and the nature

* Judicial Conference of Senior Circuit Judges, *Report of the Committee on Punishment for Crime,* pp. 26, 27 (1942).

of the enterprise—the regulation of the flow of evidence, the predictable eruption of emergencies, the endless stream of cloudy questions demanding swift answers—generate pressures for decisive action. And so the trial judge, who starts his career well along the course of a life in which self-effacement has not been the key thing, is encouraged to follow his assertive ways.

Conditioned in the direction of authoritarianism by his daily life in court, long habituated as a lawyer to the stance of the aggressive contestant, and exercising sentencing powers frequently without practical limits, the trial judge is not discouraged from venting any tendencies toward righteous arrogance. The books and the reliable folklore are filled with the resulting horror stories—of fierce sentences and orgies of denunciatory attacks upon defendants. One need not be a revolutionist or an enemy of the judiciary to predict that untrained, untested, unsupervised men armed with great power will perpetrate abuses. The horrible cases may result from moral or intellectual or physical deficiencies—or from all together. But we can be sure there will be some substantial number of such cases.

Everyone connected with this grim business has his own favorite atrocity stories. James V. Bennett, the enlightened former Director of the Federal Bureau of Prisons, wrote this often-quoted passage, which appears in a 1964 Senate Document:

> That some judges are arbitrary and even sadistic in their sentencing practices is notoriously a matter of record. By reason of senility or a virtually pathological emotional complex some judges summarily impose the maximum on defendants convicted of certain types of crimes or all types of crimes. One judge's disposition along this line was a major factor in bringing about a sitdown strike at Connecticut's Wethersfield Prison in 1956. There is one judge who, as a matter of routine, always gives the maximum sentence and who of course is avoided by

every defense lawyer. If they have the misfortune of having their case arise before him they lay the ground for appeals since experience has indicated the appeals court is sympathetic and will, if possible, overturn the sentencing court. I know of one judge who continued to sit on the bench and sentence defendants to prison while he was undergoing shock treatments for a mental illness.*

Forgoing the temptation to parade more lurid instances, I think a couple of mild, substantially colorless cases within my own ken give some sense of the unchained sentencing power in operation. One story concerns a casual anecdote over cocktails in a rare conversation among judges touching the subject of sentencing. Judge X, to designate him in a lawyerlike way, told of a defendant for whom the judge, after reading the presentence report, had decided tentatively upon a sentence of four years' imprisonment. At the sentencing hearing in the courtroom, after hearing counsel, Judge X invited the defendant to exercise his right to address the court in his own behalf. The defendant took a sheaf of papers from his pocket and proceeded to read from them, excoriating the judge, the "kangaroo court" in which he'd been tried, and the legal establishment in general. Completing the story, Judge X said, "I listened without interrupting. Finally, when he said he was through, I simply gave the son of a bitch five years instead of the four." None of the three judges listening to that (including me) tendered a whisper of dissent, let alone a scream of outrage. But think about it. Not the relatively harmless, if revealing, reference to the defendant as a son of a bitch. But a year in prison for speaking disrespectfully to a judge.** Was that, perhaps, based upon a rapid, subtle judgment that a defendant behaving this way in the courtroom

* "The Sentence—Its Relation to Crime and Rehabilitation," in *Of Prisons and Justice*. S. Doc. No. 70, 88th Cong., 2d sess., p. 311 (1964).

** Only the prissiness of a lawyer's training would require a footnote here to acknowledge that I have neglected the calculation of probable time off for good behavior.

showed insufficient evidence of remorse and prospects of reform? I confidently think not. Should defendants be warned that exercise of their "right" to address the court may be this costly? They are not.* Would we tolerate an act of Congress penalizing such an outburst by a year in prison? The question, however rhetorical, misses one truly exquisite note of agony: that the wretch sentenced by Judge X never knew, because he was never told, how the fifth year of his term came to be added.

That short story epitomizes much that prompts me to be writing this: the large and unregulated character of the sentencing power, the resulting arbitrariness permitted in its exercise, the frightening chanciness of judicial tempers and reactions. Whatever our platonic vision of the judge may be, this subject, like others, must be considered in the setting of a real world of real, mixed, fallible judicial types.

Let me turn here to my second, somewhat more appalling, anecdote. I happened a few years ago to preside at a widely publicized trial of a government official charged with corrupt behavior and perjury, convicted finally on a perjury count. While the conviction was for perjury only, the aura of corruption tended to overhang the case. In the weeks between the verdict and the sentence, as sometimes happens, I received some unsolicited mail, often vindictive in tone, not infrequently anonymous. One letter was from a more august source. A state trial judge, from Florida, wrote as follows:

Dear Judge Frankel:

I have read with interest the proceedings in the case involving above Defendant and his influence peddling, perjury, etc. . . .

* Dr. Willard Gaylin, in his work *In the Service of their Country—War Resisters in Prison* (New York, Viking Press, 1970), p. 283, reports an episode identical with mine about Judge X. There is other evidence—including, I fear, some results of my own introspection—that the defendant's rare outburst may carry a monstrous price.

One of the more serious problems confronting Judges in the State Courts, such as the one in which I preside, is the leniency extended by the Federal Judiciary and the pampering of prisoners and parolees by the Federal Penal and Parole Systems. It is difficult for me to justify giving an individual 10, 15, 20 years or life for armed robberies involving a few dollars when persons in the Federal Judicial System are usually given much smaller sentences and are paroled after having served a few months or years of their sentences, and then are proceeded to be loosely supervised by an overly compassionate and headturning parole system.

Accordingly, as an individual, as a Judge in the State Court, as a father of a young man serving upon the High Seas of the country as an enlisted man, and as the step-father of a drafted Army Private on Asiatic soil, and as an individual who has served honorably for five years in the service of the United States Navy in wartime, let me strongly urge upon you that you impose the maximum sentence as provided by law upon the above Defendant, and upon any other individuals who would tend to destroy and demoralize our nation's government from within.

The author of that letter was deeply in earnest. What he wrote was not intended as a caricature. I am sure he did not mean to document the enormities we invite when we empower untested and unqualified officials to spew wholesale sentences of "10, 15, 20 years or life for armed robberies involving a few dollars. . . ." He was not applying for the analyst's couch when he tendered up his generations of patriotism, his cruelty, and his confident ownership of ultimate truths. He was not—I assume, regretfully, he still is not—slowed for a second by any shibboleth about "individualized treatment" when he offered advice on sentencing to a fellow judge based upon newspaper intelligence, without even seeing the defendant or reading a presentence report.

What that Florida colleague did was merely to dramatize the macabre point that sweeping penalty statutes allow sentences to be "individualized" not so much in terms of defendants but mainly in terms of the wide spectrums of character, bias, neurosis, and daily vagary encountered among occupants of the trial bench. It is no wonder that wherever supposed professionals in the field—criminologists, penologists, probation officers, and, yes, lawyers and judges—discuss sentencing, the talk inevitably dwells upon the problem of "disparity." Some writers have quibbled about the definitiveness of the evidence showing disparity. It is among the least substantial of quibbles. The evidence is conclusive that judges of widely varying attitudes on sentencing, administering statutes that confer huge measures of discretion, mete out widely divergent sentences where the divergences are explainable only by the variations among the judges, not by material differences in the defendants or their crimes. Even in our age of science and skepticism, the conclusion would seem to be among those still acceptable as self-evident. What would require proof of a weighty kind, and something astonishing in the way of theoretical explanation, would be the suggestion that assorted judges, subject to little more than their own unfettered wills, could be expected to impose consistent sentences. In any event, if proof were needed that sentences vary simply because judges vary, there is plenty of it. The evidence grows every time judges gather to discuss specific cases and compare notes on the sentences they would impose upon given defendants. The disparities, if they are no longer astonishing, remain horrible.

The broad experience of former Prison Director Bennett merits another quotation here from the 1964 Senate Document mentioned earlier:

> Take, for instance, the cases of two men we received last spring. The first man had been convicted of cashing a check for $58.40. He was out of work at the time of his offense, and when his

wife became ill and he needed money for rent, food, and doctor bills, he became the victim of temptation. He had no prior criminal record. The other man cashed a check for $35.20. He was also out of work and his wife had left him for another man. His prior record consisted of a drunk charge and a nonsupport charge. Our examination of these two cases indicated no significant differences for sentencing purposes. But they appeared before different judges and the first man received 15 years in prison and the second man 30 days.

These are not cases picked out of thin air. In January the President of the United States commuted to time served the sentence of a first offender, a former Army lieutenant, and a veteran of over 500 days in combat, who had been given 18 years for forging six small checks.

In one of our institutions a middle-aged credit union treasurer is serving 117 days for embezzling $24,000 in order to cover his gambling debts. On the other hand, another middle-aged embezzler with a fine past record and a fine family is serving 20 years, with 5 years probation to follow. At the same institution is a war veteran, a 39-year-old attorney who has never been in trouble before, serving 11 years for illegally importing parrots into this country. Another who is destined for the same institution is a middle-aged tax accountant who on tax fraud charges received 31 years and 31 days in consecutive sentences. In stark contrast, at the same institution last year an unstable young man served out his 98-day sentence for armed bank robbery.*

Protesting more than enough, let me say again that the tragic state of disorder in our sentencing practices is not attributable to any unique endowments of sadism or bestiality among judges as a species. Without claiming absolute detachment, I am prepared to hypothesize that judges in general, if only because of occupational conditioning, may be somewhat calmer, more dispassionate, and more humane than the

* "Countdown for Judicial Sentencing" in *Of Prisons and Justice*. S. Doc. No. 70, 88th Cong., 2d sess., p. 331 (1964).

average of people across the board. But nobody has the experience of being sentenced by "judges in general." The particular defendant on some existential day confronts a specific judge. The occupant of the bench on that day may be punitive, patriotic, self-righteous, guilt-ridden, and more than customarily dyspeptic. The vice in our system is that all such qualities have free rein as well as potentially fatal impact upon the defendant's finite life.

Such individual, personal powers are not evil only, or mainly, because evil people may come to hold positions of authority. The more pervasive wrong is that a regime of substantially limitless discretion is by definition arbitrary, capricious, and antithetical to the rule of law. Some judges I know believe (and act on the belief) that all draft resisters should receive the maximum sentence, five years; this iron view rests variously upon calculations concerning time off for good behavior, how long those in uniform serve, how contemptible it is to refuse military service, etc. Other judges I know have thought, at least lately, that persons opposing service on grounds of moral or other principle, even if technically guilty of a felony, should be subjected to token terms in prison, or none at all. It is not directly pertinent here whether either category of judge is right, or whether both have failed to exercise, case by case, the discretion with which the law entrusts them. The simple point at the moment is the contrast between such individual, personal, conflicting criteria and the ideal of the rule of law.

Beyond the random spreads of judicial attitudes, there is broad latitude in our sentencing laws for kinds of class bias that are commonly known, never explicitly acknowledged, and at war with the superficial neutrality of the statute as literally written. Judges are on the whole more likely to have known personally tax evaders, or people just like tax evaders, than car thieves or dope pushers. Dichotomies of a similar kind are obvious beyond the need to multiply examples. Can such items of personal experience fail to have effects upon sentencing? I do not stop at simpleminded observations about the substantial numbers of judges who simply do not impose prison sentences for tax evasion though the federal law, for example, provides a maximum of five years per count (and tax-evasion prosecutions frequently involve several tax years, with each a separate count). There are more things at stake than judicial "bias" when tax evaders average relatively rare and brief prison terms, while more frequent and much longer average terms (under a statute carrying the same five-year maximum) are imposed for interstate transport of stolen motor vehicles.* Whatever other factors may be operating, however, it is not possible to avoid the impression that the judges' private senses of good and evil are playing significant parts no matter what the law on the books may define as the relative gravity of the several crimes. And, although it anticipates a later subject, this is certainly the focus of the familiar jailhouse complaint that "the more you steal, the less of a sentence you get." I believe the complaint has a basis in the fundamental realities and in the way justice is seen to be dispensed. The latter aspect is important in itself; among our sounder aphorisms is the one teaching that justice must not only be done, but must appear to be done. Both objectives are missed by a system leaving to individual preferences and value judgments the kind of discretion our judges have over sentencing.

I have touched upon individual traits of temperament and variations of an ideological, political, or social character. The

* It may serve only to confirm a priori hunches, but consider these illustrative figures for federal sentences in the fiscal year 1969. Of 502 defendants convicted for income tax fraud, 95, or 19 percent, received prison terms, the average term being three months. Of 3,791 defendants sentenced for auto theft, 2,373, or 63 percent, went to prison, the average term being 7.6 months. From the Administrative Office of the U.S. Courts' publication, *Federal Offenders in the United States District Courts,* 1969, pp. 146–7 (1971).

sentencing power is so far unregulated that even matters of a relatively technical, seemingly "legal" nature are left for the individual judge, and thus for whimsical handling, at least in the sense that no two judges need be the same. Should a defendant be deemed to deserve some leniency if he has pled guilty rather than going to trial? Many judges say yes; many, perhaps a minority, say no; all do as they please. Should a prior criminal record enhance punishment? Most judges seem to think so. Some take the view that having "paid the price" for prior offenses, the defendant should not pay again now. Again, dealer's choice. Many judges believe it a mitigating factor if defendant yields to the pressure, moral or other, to pay back what he has taken. Others condemn this view as an illicit use of criminal sanctions for private redress. Once more, no rule of law enforces either of these contradictory judgments. There are other illustrations —relating, for example, to family conditions, defendant's behavior at trial, the consideration, if any, for turning state's evidence—all subject to the varying and unregulated views of judges. The point is, I hope, sufficiently made that our sentencing judgments splay wildly as results of unpredictable and numerous variables embodied in the numerous and variegated inhabitants of our trial benches.

Among the articles of wisdom for which we honor those who wrote the American Constitution was the keen concern to test all powers by the possibility of having wicked or otherwise unsound men in office. In this realistic light, it was deemed vital to confine power as much as possible and to hedge it about with checking and balancing powers. Like everything, such precautions can be overdone. But we have lost sight of them almost entirely, and without justification, in our sweeping grants of sentencing authority.

3

The Dubious Process

IN DISCUSSING the wide powers given to judges and the qualifications of those exercising the powers, I have touched here and there upon aspects of the sentencing procedure in operation. But it seems worthwhile to sketch a somewhat more coherent account of the process. For some basic problems inhere in, or are disclosed by, the mechanics and the rituals with which criminal penalties are adjudged. The outline followed here reflects the federal practice, and specifically that in the Southern District of New York, with which I am directly familiar. The essential features are fairly standard, however. To the extent (which is considerable) that I am accentuating the negative, reliance upon the federal model does not unduly blacken the general picture. It is widely agreed (and it would be silly to affect modesty about this) that federal practices in sentencing and corrections equal or excel the best of those in the states.

Under the philosophy and practice of individualized sentencing which still prevails, it is necessary to study and somehow characterize or classify each defendant before he may be sentenced. This is the most rational and least debatable tenet of contemporary sentencing doctrine. Accordingly, the defendant who has pled, or been found, guilty is assigned to a probation officer for presentence investigation. The report embodying the results of this investigation will give an account of the offense, the defendant, defendant's prior record, family, work, strengths, and weaknesses. The purposes of such an account are clear enough. Problems arise in the implementation and detailed elaboration of those purposes. The problems spring from the specific nature of the information sought, the personnel and techniques for seeking it, and the standard attitudes reflected in the use of the data.

The presentence investigation represents a sudden and total departure from the fact-gathering procedures the court has employed up to that point. The defendant, shielded before by his privilege against self-incrimination, now becomes the first and most obvious source to be tapped. This makes sense—but with important limitations that are often not enforced or even perceived. Among the most clearly relevant questions are those relating to the circumstances and details of the defendant's crime. The defendant, now convicted, is a first source of the information. This usually creates no difficulty where the defendant has pled guilty or plans no appeal from his conviction. But the defendant who does plan to appeal is confronted with a dilemma which the investigator and the judge are frequently unwilling to modify. If the defendant tells all, he may eviscerate his pending appeal or the new trial he hopes to win. If he insists on protesting his innocence, he is likely to be tagged for lacking the remorse or repentance that is commonly thought vital in considering mitigation. If he refuses to talk altogether, he is in a similar box. The quandary exists as a procedural matter because the sentence, being technically and otherwise the judgment of conviction, precedes the appeal. Like most man-made quandaries, it is manageable by men: for example, the sentencing judge may acknowledge the defendant's plight, impose sentence despite defendant's silence or "obstinacy," but offer to reconsider if and when the conviction becomes final after appeals. But that course is not commonly followed, or considered, and it generates annoying problems of its own.

By way of fuller disclosure, let me report that I tried the suggested technique in the case of an especially difficult sentence, where the defendant had plausible grounds for appeal, refused to concede anything to the probation officer, and seemed, among other things, to be concealing much information about wrongdoing by himself and others. As things stood at the time of sentencing, I thought there might be reason to reduce the term being imposed if and when the defendant should feel able to speak freely. I said this, inviting him to apply for reduction of sentence after affirmance of the conviction, if that occurred. The conviction was affirmed, and the defendant did make a later application. But his purpose was not to tell anything; instead, he claimed that the procedure I'd followed was an unlawful attempt to force him to talk, violating his privilege against self-incrimination. The argument may have been debatable, but it was rejected, generating still another unsuccessful appeal. The episode reflects at least the awkwardness of switching after guilt is determined from the strictly adversary mode to the kind of inquisitorial process required if the effort to individualize sentences is to be manageable at all without wildly prohibitive investments of time and resources.

Whether or not the defendant's own knowledge is available without inhibition, he is not the only source (or certainly reliable source) of information about his criminal misconduct. Much of what the probation officer learns about the crime directly involved and about defendant's prior record he obtains from the prosecutor's office. That twangs another of the adversary lawyer's most sensitive nerves. The ex parte reports, under existing law, seem perfectly legal for sentencing purposes. It does not follow that Anglo-American defense lawyers will be entirely comfortable about this. And the uneasiness has some basis. The prosecutor's files often tell that the bank robbery for which defendant awaits sentence is only the latest in a series, the prior ones not having been formally provable for one "technical" reason or another. A good deal of other damaging information may be acquired in this fashion. Much of the information may be accurate. Much may not. None, or almost none, will be exposed to adversary scrutiny, to rechecking at sources, to cross-examination, and to final evaluation by an impartial third party after opposing lawyers have torn at the material and at each other about it.

To "try" such matters in the full sense is a practical impossibility. To exclude them for that reason is unacceptable. There is no perfect compromise. The possible direction of some accommodation is suggested below.

The probation officer continues beyond the prosecutor's office his ex parte investigations for the presentence report. With varying limits of time, energy, and concern for potential injury to people and relationships, the officer will make inquiries of schools, employers, associates, neighbors, pastors, friends, enemies. All kinds of untested assertions and impressions, not always impersonal or lacking in ulterior purposes, may in this way filter into the officer's ken and his resulting report. Seasoned, sensitive officers are alert to such factors. The best of them—of us—are not capable of panning only the accurate and reliable information from ores of this nature. Again, however, if we are to learn about the defendant, these sources must be explored and the orthodox procedures of the courtroom must be largely or wholly bypassed.

The omission of standard trial techniques for developing evidence may be partially offset by allowing the defense to see the presentence report and contest claimed inaccuracies. How the contest should or would be conducted is a question not simply answered. But before reaching it, I must note that there is bitter disagreement over whether disclosure to the defense should be made at all. Most probation officers and many, if not most, judges in my experience (casual, not Gallup) are against disclosure. The reasons have a sound familiar from other areas of claimed confidentiality, though that does not signify they lack substance. It is argued that informants will hesitate or refuse to tell what they know if their reports are not kept in confidence. It is also asserted that the relaxed, mutually trusting relationship between the probation officer and the judge will stiffen if the officer's account becomes a kind of public document. In this same vein, there is a fear that the presentence report will itself become a new subject for extended litigation—because the judge has agreed with it (thus being a "rubber stamp," failing to exercise his discretion) or disagreed with it (showing he does not know what he's doing) or was otherwise influenced by it in allegedly illicit respects.

These arguments have some weight. And there is no certain conclusion applicable across the board. The confidential informant is, of course, a menacing and dangerous creature. He plays, nevertheless, an ancient, and not uniformly dishonorable, role in law enforcement. In the flesh, moreover, he may be more appealing than sinister. Consider, for example, a case of mine involving a persistent, hardened, violent criminal about whom it was difficult to learn anything ostensibly favorable. The only item inconsistent with his general pattern of wickedness was his report of tender devotion to his wife, confirmed by her in his presence to the probation officer. The probation officer also reported that the wife had later come to see him alone, expressing unqualified hatred of the defendant and explaining that she had lied earlier because her husband, repeatedly and violently assaultive, had threatened to kill her if she did otherwise. The officer suggested that I grant the wife's request to see her alone. I did. She confirmed, in seemingly great fear, what the probation officer had given as her true views. She documented the tales of violence with police and court records. I believed her. It remains possible she was perpetrating a clever pattern of falsehoods. Should I, in any event, have compelled her to tell her story on the record? Or should I have disclosed what she had said to the defendant? Or should I have attempted, with whatever success, to "strike" her ex parte testimony and cause it to play no part in the sentencing? I do not suggest these are easy questions. I do not tender my negative answers to them as certainly correct. I merely give the example as some evidence that the attractive idea of full disclosure at all times may be excessive.

The governing federal rules, like the practice of many states, leave the decision on disclosure to the discretion of the trial judge. The discretion, as I have indicated, tends to be exercised usually to deny disclosure. This is, in my view, another of the many cases of seemingly good rules that don't work well. I tend to think the matter should lie in discretion, but a discretion closely confined. There are cases where revelations would do much more harm than good. It is not feasible to predict such situations by a formula. Generally, however, our judicial tradition of putting things "on the record" is the safe, fair, and salutary way to proceed. My own suggestion, based upon these premises, is that disclosure ought to be the preferred and presumed rule, subject only to exceptions for rare and unique cases where the judge perceives specific dangers or injuries to be avoided.

A familiar consequence of putting things on the record is that it generates disputes. If the defendant and his lawyer are told the negative items in the presentence report, we can expect confidently that at least many such assertions will be controverted. That raises the specter of trial after trial in a criminal process that is already too slow. But it is no answer, obviously, to conclude that the contents of presentence reports must be accepted with no contest or question. The things we think we must "know" to sentence someone ought to be true as much of the time as possible. It may be that we attempt to know more than is fair or helpful for this purpose. Part of the remedy is to eliminate extraneous and prejudicial information. As to matters that are germane, we should be able to evolve procedures short of a full-blown formal trial for hearing conflicting evidence and making findings on more than the ex parte hearsay now comprising much of our presentence reports. I will not attempt a detailed prescription here. It is enough to observe that we have figured out in various kinds of administrative and judicial proceedings how to abbreviate standard trial procedures without sacrificing the basic right to confront and counter adverse assertions.

What ought to be perfectly clear at any rate is the intolerable risk of error when we rely for grave decisions of law upon untested hearsay and rumor. Our trial procedures eschewing such reliance presumably rest upon the solid experience of centuries both in and out of court. We should have learned from repeated examples the dangers of secret "facts" from unnamed informers. But we continue to operate in our sentencing practice as if we had no such learning. And the damage we do as a result is in its nature hidden and "incalculable" in more senses than one. Occasionally, the lid is opened and appalling things are revealed. Once in a while, the revelations are even spread onto the pages of the law reports, though their effects are thus far unnoticeable.

A reported case in point was decided in 1960 by the Appellate Division of New Jersey's Superior Court.* The defendant—a man of twenty-six, married, with two children, who had stolen a car when he was eighteen and had one or two other collisions with the criminal law—was sentenced in 1951 on what amounted to a guilty plea to charges of forging seven checks totaling $1,467. With each forgery constituting legally a separate crime, though all were part of a single series of forgeries on a single occasion, he was sentenced to seven

* *State* v. *Pohlabel*. 61 N.J. Super. 242, 160 A.2d 647 (1960).

consecutive terms of three to five years, or a total of twenty-one to thirty-five years. In the decision reported nine years later, it finally came out that the presentence report had erroneously stated (or said things leading the sentencing judge to think erroneously) that the defendant had lived a "life of crime," had "spent the greater part of his life" in prison, had received a life term in California, and was being left by the relieved California authorities to be dealt with appropriately in New Jersey. A New Jersey parole officer, a Mr. Dragon (*sic*), departing from the usual (and lawful) practice, volunteered a recommendation for a maximum sentence. All this poison, which is the central point here, had been administered privately to the sentencing judge without disclosure to —and so without opportunity for correction by—defendant or his lawyer. And it had taken nine years for the defendant to unlock the concealed mistakes, which entitled him at last, not to be released but to be resentenced without reference to the false reports and unfounded recommendation. Whether or not this might be sickening enough, we should reckon on the fact that Mr. Pohlabel's case (see preceding footnote) is undoubtedly a rare exception among the many in which nobody ever finds out about tragic errors of a similar nature.

To move on that note from our deficient techniques of fact-gathering, there is a troublesome quality of class bias both in the subjects treated in foresentence reports and the standard modes of treatment. For example, defendant's religion, or lack of it, is a regular topic. The typical entry on religion is terse, unsubtle, and heavily weighted toward swift orthodoxy in judgment, viz.:

> The defendant was reared as a Roman Catholic, but claims only occasional church attendance since his high school graduation.

The implication of such reported "facts" seems clear enough on the face of the reports. It tends to be re-enforced when the subject is (as it rarely is in my experience) discussed with the probation officer. Most such officers, whether from conventional biases or from ostensibly social-scientific premises, deem church attendance a favorable fact and non-attendance unfavorable. The hypothesis may have some vague and slender merit. But it is treated with hasty superficiality. There is not time, and commonly not talent, enough to explore nice questions as to the moral environment of the defendant and his family. Beyond the dangerous hypothesis that religiosity connotes morality, there is no exploration of the infinite complexities that would need scrutiny before attempting useful judgments about the essentially moral qualities of the individual facing sentence. Given the bland treatment now accorded it, the subject of religion would probably be better omitted altogether from presentence reports.

The tendency toward a rather simplistic conventionality, and some fundamental hostility toward defendants, reveals itself in other ways. The standard jargon is one. Defendants intimate with, but not married to, members of the other sex have "paramours." If the intimacy extends to living together, they have "meretricious relationships." If they are asked whether they use narcotics and say no, they "deny" the use of narcotics. Other forms of common misbehavior are similarly "denied," whereas (presumably) the questions about such misbehavior simply do not arise with respect to Senator X or Father Y or Judge Z.

The generally orthodox probation officer, addressing the generally orthodox judge, relies heavily upon orthodox and official sources. As I have mentioned, much that appears in the presentence report originates from the prosecutor or the prosecutor's files and is passed on with little or no independent scrutiny. The result is a good deal of "raw" data, not rendered pure or more reliable by being recounted as unqualified "fact."

Official housing arrangements and lines of authority reenforce the qualities of establishmentism in the process of investigation and study preceding sentence. Probation officers, prosecutors, and judges tend to work in the same or adjoining buildings. Government counsel "represent" the probation office when it proceeds against, or is proceeded against by, defendants. The "official" people are habituated to confer and identify with each other. The defense lawyer, though he is often an ex-prosecutor, is physically and spiritually "outside." The defendant is, of course, much farther outside and alien.

I have, in this brief and non-technical account, sketched only some of the disquieting aspects of our individual studies to make the sentence fit the defendant. Even so, I have dwelt morbidly upon the dark side because, here and throughout, my concern is with what I perceive as deep troubles. Nevertheless, for a modicum of balance, I should tarry over some matters of substance on the other side. Having worked with and relied heavily upon them for so long, I could not fail to testify to the large number of probation officers who are concerned, sensitive, and committed to their tough assignments. It is vital, also, to realize that whatever its defects, the presentence investigation is indispensable in any sentencing scheme that does not treat the infinite varieties of people as entirely fungible. This means, in my workaday terms, that we could not pretend at all to any measure of sense in sentencing without the basic presentence investigation. Moreover, if my remarks about conventionality sound smug, let it be said there is no ground whatever for that. The judges are surely not less conventional than the probation officers. On the contrary, it seems probable that sentences would be wilder and stiffer than they are without the steadying influence of probation officers. The judges, for whom criminal defendants are part-time and relatively recent phenomena, might well be disposed, at least in their early years on the bench, toward shocked and punitive reactions. The probation officers, literally case-hardened, are likely on the whole to be more understanding and balanced.

This last thought is not belied by the fact that judges seem more often to reduce than to increase (where they change at all) sentences recommended by probation officers. Despite our extensive cruelties, our society professes devotion to gentleness and mercy. And there is a pressure in interpersonal affairs toward the virtuous stance. This, rather than any special store of gentleness, probably explains why the judge considering a recommendation is likely to lean prima facie toward a show of leniency. Other pressures may overbalance or neutralize this. But the pressure is there and would operate similarly if the positions were reversed. I think, that is, that the probation officer would tend to reduce more often than he increased if it were his role to state the decision after the judge had offered the recommendation.

Let us return to the character of the sentencing process, to the point where the presentence report, however flawed, is ready for the judge. The judge reads the report and may or may not confer thereafter with the probation officer. Either way, I infer from a good deal of reliable circumstantial evidence that the process is not long in the usual case. Confessing for myself, and making inferences from the schedules of other judges, I doubt that the total time for such study (including conference with the probation officer) exceeds half an hour in the case of the average defendant.

However slowly or quickly, the judge reaches at this stage some tentative sentence, which is probably the sentence later imposed in 90 percent or so of all the cases. There remains, however, the formal proceeding in the courtroom.

As I have observed earlier, that proceeding is truly a formality in most cases. Its organization and design are not calculated to make it anything else very often. The prosecutor in my court almost never has anything to say.* Occasionally, he reports that defendant has "cooperated" (given evidence against others), which is to be considered in his favor. Sometimes the prosecutor speaks of the gravity of the crime and other evidence of defendant's bad character. In the courts of New York and other states, this kind of denunciatory presentation, ending in a plea for a stern sentence, is more common than it is in my court. Whichever is the standard style, the prosecuting attorney rarely supplies any semblance of a full, rounded account upon which a rational sentence could be founded.

The standard presentation by defense counsel is different, but not much more useful. It is in the nature of things a plea for a light sentence. The defense lawyer, perhaps inevitably, sees his purpose as avoiding imprisonment of his client, or keeping the term as short as possible. Defining his advocate's role in these simple terms, he rarely considers whether some form of custodial treatment, however unattractive it looks to the defendant, might actually be the most hopeful course for the defendant in the long run. The usual defense lawyer's statement pleads for compassion, stressing the defendant's virtues, if any; family ties; the good opinions of clerics, employers, teachers, and the like. Such things are relevant, to be sure. They appear, however, to be neither novel nor wholly accurate to the judge who has read the presentence report. They are, at any rate, the best most defense attorneys can muster. Again, as in the case of the prosecutors, there are exceptions. An occasional lawyer for the defense has made the sentencing problem a subject of genuine study; has managed effectively to size up the judge and his concerns; and succeeds in proposing an appropriate, imaginative, and sensible sentence that appears genuinely to serve both the cli-

* As this is written, there is pressure from some of the judges, including me, to change this aloof stance.

ent's and the public's interests. This is not—in our existing system it probably could not be—at all common.

When the lawyers are through, defendant is in most courts given an opportunity to speak for himself. I have mentioned this stage, including both the most common defendant, who mumbles a useless word or says nothing; the very rare one, who orates at length; and the danger here that the rewards of the oration will be a stiffer sentence than might otherwise have been imposed. Speaking once more of the usual case, defendant's turn in the spotlight is fleeting and inconsequential.

With the oral presentations completed, the judge almost always announces the sentence instantly. This is so familiar that few of us ever wonder about the practice, let alone deviate from it. Yet it bears some wondering about. The sentence is so grave a matter—so much more solemn and awful than most things courts do. For matters of relative triviality, the lawyers write and talk more, and the judge rarely decides on the spot, "from the bench."

My point, a somewhat repetitious one, is not that the proceeding, in the present state of law and learning, ought to take longer. My point is that there is rarely, if ever, much to take longer *about*. Because there are virtually no rules or tests or standards—and thus no issues to resolve—there is little occasion to talk or think. The judgment is swift because the process of reaching it is not reflective or orderly. The court renders no "opinion" because it has not followed the rational steps required to create one.

The speed and the brevity are, in my view, symptoms of the basic malady. But they become, as I suggest in the following chapter, substantial causes in themselves of much further malfunctioning and misery in the corrections process.

4

Walls of Silence

THE QUESTION "Why?" states a primitive and insistent human need. The small child, punished or deprived, demands an explanation. The existence of a rationale may not make the hurt pleasant, or even just. But the absence, or refusal, of reasons is a hallmark of injustice. So it requires no learning in law or political philosophy to apprehend that the swift ukase, without explanation, is the tyrant's way. The despot is not bound by rules. He need not justify or account for what he does.

Criminal sentences, as our judges commonly pronounce them, are in these vital respects tyrannical. Largely unfettered by limiting standards, and thus having neither occasion nor meaningful terms for explaining, the judge usually supplies nothing in the way of a coherent and rational judgment when he informs the defendant of his fate. A similar void, a similar pattern of stark commands and decrees, pervades the whole course of "corrections." It is among the most galling and dehumanizing aspects of the process.

Atrocious as it may seem, this swift and unreasoned form of decree is widely accepted without question. We expect the judge to rule "from the bench," as the general expression goes—i.e., to pronounce sentence immediately after he hears counsel and the defendant. We expect—perhaps prefer—that he should simply state the sentence, with no explanation or "opinion" to speak of. But these are, if we think about them, rather extraordinary expectations. In most matters of any difficulty, the judge does not rule from the bench. He reads briefs, then hears oral argument, then "reserves decision" for days or weeks or months, during some of which he is presumably studying and thinking. Furthermore, however much or little thought it may reflect, an opinion, an explanation of the result, is expected for most final determinations in either judicial or quasi-judicial proceedings.

So, for example, in the federal courts and many states, when a judge tries a civil case without a jury, he is expected to spell out, normally in writing, what he finds as facts and what legal conclusions he rests upon such findings. The requirement applies to all manner of cases—including such matters as who is liable for the bent fender, who breached the contract for a shipment of overalls, or who copied the dress design from whom. I have given examples intended not to sound momentous. But, of course, such disputes are not trivial either, certainly not to the disputants. The point, anyhow, is that the parties (especially the loser) are, on deep principles, not merely entitled to a decision; they are entitled to an explanation. And this serves for more than the satisfaction of aesthetic or purely spiritual needs, though I disclaim any belittling of these. The duty to give an account of the decision is to promote thought by the decider, to compel him to cover the relevant points, to help him eschew irrelevancies—and, finally, to make him show that these necessities have been served. The requirement of reasons expressly stated is not a guarantee of fairness. The judge or other official may give good reasons while he acts upon outrageous ones. However, given decision-makers who are both tolerably honest and normally fallible, the requirement of stated reasons is a powerful safeguard against rash and arbitrary decisions.

Knowing this to be so, we apply it to affairs of clearly lesser consequence, yet we place no burden of explanation upon the judge who decides that the defendant before him must be locked up for ten years rather than five or one or none. The judge thus loosed may be one of the world's most virtuous people. Or he may not. In either event, he is not encouraged or even invited to proceed according to law. He may be propelled toward a stern sentence by high moral values or by private quirks of a less elegant nature or by a perceived affront to his dignity in the courtroom. Whatever accounts for his judgment, he need not say, and he normally does not say.

It is certain beyond question that a power this wild will spawn at least some results that are bizarre and would be promptly condemned as unlawful if the unspoken grounds of decision were known. If this certainty requires proof, every criminal lawyer knows cases in which sentencing judges have done crazy and horrible things. Some such cases, only a few, even find their way into the law books. I have mentioned the instances, probably more numerous than we like to imagine, in which insolence has been punished beyond tolerable measure. A prosecutor recently told of a federal judge who explained on the record that the defendant had behaved like a seventeen-year-old, not like the man of twenty-four he was, so that he should be, and was, sentenced to a prison term of seven years. Another federal judge—supposedly bound to exercise subtle discretion and to "individualize" sentences—announced that the defendant before him (and any other), charged with armed robbery, pleading not guilty, demanding a jury trial, and then being convicted, would get life.

The last of these examples (it would be simple work to fill a large book with others) is a reported case in which the trial judge, having explained his judgment, was reversed on appeal.* He earned the reversal because he announced his position, and what he said showed that he was acting by a rigid (and wrong) "rule," rather than exercising lawful discretion. This is, to repeat what was just said in a footnote, a most extraordinary kind of happening. Since, as I have said, judges usually say little or nothing to explain their sentences, the possibility that they were moved by absurd or vicious considerations is not usually open to inquiry. And the circle proceeds to be closed. The judges, if they are merely human rather than depraved, do not enjoy being caught in error. They know that an unexplained decision does not flaunt its possible fallacies. When they are not required to explain, many at least find this conclusive grounds for not explaining. There is no way of knowing, then, how many sentences, for how many thousands of years, have rested upon hidden premises that could not have survived scrutiny.

Such mysteries invite fevered imaginings or shrewd guesses. It is widely rumored or suspected that severity or leniency in sentencing may be influenced by racial or religious prejudices, by the personal experiences of individual judges with particular kinds of crime, and by other forms of hidden bias lacking any title to legality.** The absence of any explanation

* In Chapter 7, I criticize the law in the federal courts and most states making sentences substantially unreviewable on appeal. Unreviewability is indeed the rule rather than the exception, so that an appellate court will not even consider whether a sentence, if within the statutory maximum, might be thought in some sense to be "excessive." The point just made in the text touches only an exceedingly rare and accidental type of exception. If a judge (1) sentenced a man severely for being a Baptist or having long hair or (as with the example in the text) for exercising his right to jury trial and (2) was careless enough to expose such real and bizarre reasons, he could then be reversed because he would, in legal parlance, have gone beyond the bounds of even the sweeping discretion he has over sentences.

** I have mentioned earlier (in Chapter 2) the knowledgeable observations of James V. Bennett concerning the impact of judicial idiosyncrasies upon sentences. Every criminal lawyer and candid judge could add to the roster of horribles. If it is not all tabulated in neat statistics, there is familiar evidence that race and class prejudice, personal views about specific crimes, or purported justification for the sentence is among the more familiar and understandable sources of bitterness among people in prison. Philosophers have agreed for ages on the ideal that the person suffering punishment should be guided to understand and, in the ultimate hope, realize the justice of the affliction. Our practice of terse dispositions is at the opposite pole. The baleful results are aggravated when prisoners come to compare their unexplained sentences and perceive intimately what the scholars mean by disparity. As I have said, irrational disparities are real and pervasive. But even where these are not, in fact, baseless distinctions—even, that is, where differences in sentence could be justified by relevant differences in the cases—the possible justification is unknown and unavailing. The prisoner is not powerfully driven to magnify his own wrong. He is likely to see readily the factors that make his case proper for no more, very likely

deformed notions of patriotism, and all sorts of individual quirks affect sentences. There are powerful indications that, in general, at least in large areas of the country, black people have drawn harsher sentences than whites for essentially similar crimes in essentially comparable circumstances.

Several of the Justices in the Supreme Court's 1972 decision outlawing capital punishment (as then administered) made observations highly pertinent here. Mr. Justice Marshall wrote that

> a look at the bare statistics regarding executions is enough to betray much of the discrimination. A total of 3,859 persons have been executed since 1930, of whom 1,751 were white and 2,066 were Negro. . . . It is immediately apparent that Negroes were executed far more often than whites in proportion to their percentage of the population. Studies indicate that while the higher rate of execution among Negroes is partially due to a higher rate of crime, there is evidence of racial discrimination. . . . There is also overwhelming evidence that the death penalty is employed against men and not women. . . . It also is evident that the burden of capital punishment falls upon the poor, the ignorant, and the underprivileged members of society.

Mr. Justice Douglas, Mr. Justice Powell, and the Chief Justice (the latter two dissenting) said things reflecting at least a history of racial and other discriminations. See *Furman* v. *Georgia,* 408 U.S. 238, 364–6, 249–51, 255–7, 446–50, and 389–90, footnote 12.

less, punishment than the next man's. The splatter of varied sentences, with the unexplained variations left to be seen as random or worse, nourishes the view that there is no justice in the law.

The prevalence of this resentful outlook is attested by prisoners themselves, by attentive jailers, and by other students of the subject. More than one writer has taught that the hope of rehabilitating offenders is blighted at the inception by this rankling sense of injustice. But the remedy still lies in the future. The rudimentary decency of explaining the sentence, however briefly, is still neither required nor practiced in most cases.

The train of unhappy consequences of the unexplained sentence extends beyond the direct impact upon the defendant himself. The whole system of corrections, from sentence to parole, being so largely empty of communicable rationalities, is shrouded in silence and filled with barriers between those who should be talking and collaborating with each other. The prison officials, to whom the sentencer's views might often be pertinent, are almost never told what those views, if any, are. The kind of treatment or study the prisoner should have might turn upon the reasons for the imprisonment. But the reasons are unknown. The habit of groping in the silent dark becomes more ludicrous as the need to communicate becomes more explicit and patent.

As an example from the federal system, consider the practice under a seemingly enlightened law. We have a statute under which the judge, seeking to understand the defendant better before sentencing, may send the defendant for a "complete study" and a "report" covering all manner of biographical, physical, mental, and emotional data.* The broad categories of reportable subjects cannot be covered fully within the time (and, probably, the talents) of those entrusted with the task. The judge, I am credibly informed, normally fails

* 18 U.S.C. §4208(b) and (c).

to put specific questions that might narrow and focus the study. Responding in kind to the vague requests, those reporting on the study often supply bland generalities that add little, if anything, to the presentence reports. The inadequacy is not mitigated by the appending of diagnostic charts and summaries that are sometimes legible, and less often intelligible, to the sentencing judge.

My own favorite among the grimly amusing reports of this kind concerned an obviously disturbed, inadequate, and troublesome man who had called the F.B.I. to tell (accurately) the train he was taking to Washington to assassinate the President. Seemingly "competent" legally despite his imprudence, he pled guilty to a charge carrying a maximum possible prison sentence of up to five years. The report I had requested confirmed that he was disturbed and troublesome, told other things I already knew, and concluded that, "giving serious weight to the nature of the offense and primarily for this reason," the defendant should be given the maximum sentence under the statute. Of course, if there was anything for which the sentencing judge would not be looking to psychologists and other experts outside the law, it was guidance as to "the nature of the offense." Undoubtedly, the vagueness of my inquiry merited no more than this useless response. I have tried since to do better. Sometimes, but rarely, the reports are more helpful.

While it is not a field in which I can claim daily contact or expertise, I am reliably informed that prison officials carry forward the judges' pattern of cryptic taciturnity. The informants I describe as reliable are letter writers I have sentenced, articulate prisoners who have published their observations, and students of the subject. All describe a regime in which the machinery of degradation includes an evidently purposeful withholding of the most rudimentary and essential kinds of information. Prisoners are kept in the dark about how to behave, about what the rules (if any) are, about what in general is expected of them. They suffer not only the agonies of ignorance but recurrent evidence (or what seems such) that their keepers positively deceive and mislead them. Some suspicions of deception must reflect the inevitable paranoia that flourishes in a climate of mystery. Some of the suspicions rest undoubtedly upon fact. Whatever the proportions, the basic reality is the silence and the disdainful secrecy affected by officials who are often frightened, insecure, and ignorant themselves.

Like all walls, the barrier of non-communication has two sides. The failure or refusal of officials to tell prisoners where they stand supplies the seed and the soil for the growth of fierce inmate "governments." The "law" the authorities fail to supply is made and enforced by prisoner hierarchies. These underground powers, with their swift and ruthless sanctions, seem to be widely tolerated, if not welcomed, by many in the official prison establishment. The wielders of convict power derive and maintain their authority, at least in part, from their control of information. The familiar prison commandment, "Never talk to a screw," may sound like a tenet of rank-and-file pride. More realistically, it serves as a weapon of convict autocrats against a convict populace that must look to them for the rudimentary kind of orientation essential to a grip on sanity.

This picture may be in the process of some slow change. In a few jurisdictions, it has come to be thought that people in prison are entitled to at least some guidance—in the nature of stated rules and even conceded "rights"—by which to pattern their lives. The courts, oddly enough, have begun to enforce this idea as a matter of constitutional law. It may be that the motes thus detected by the judges may lead to the discernment of beams closer to home. In any event, while there is movement, its pace is scarcely so swift that the prison problem I have mentioned may be thought to be near extinction.

Improvements in communications are less perceptible—they are practically nonexistent—when we move on to the parole stage. It is widely, but not correctly, supposed that judges tell meaningful things to parole boards. It is clearer still that parole boards tell little or nothing to prisoners or judges. The prisoners, never guided through the supposed theories of parole, often are led to the belief that judges play a part in parole decisions. At least in the federal courts this is wholly inaccurate. Judges lack entirely the expert knowledge and continuing study of inmates on which parole boards are presumed to act. The Federal Board of Parole, evidently committed to this presumption, almost never asks a judge to express a view about parole. Yet federal prisoners write constantly to the judges who sentenced them for help in making parole. And, astonishingly, the Board of Parole encourages the flow down this blind alley.

In a booklet for prisoners republished in 1971, *You and the Parole Board,* the board reports that "The U.S. Attorney who prosecuted your case *and the Federal judge who sentenced you* are invited to make recommendations regarding parole . . ." (My italics.) Having sentenced since late 1965 more hundreds of people than I am keen to count, I can report that I have never once been so "invited." A poll among some dozens of federal trial judges produces similar reports, with exceptions too few and rare to mention. I have sought in vain for some satisfactory explanation of this blatantly misleading "information." It is not, surely, because parole-board members are more villainous as a class than judges or others. Perhaps the explanation lies close to the fact that there is no habit or duty of the parole officials to inform prisoners of anything. In this state of affairs, it is easy, and maybe congenial, to pad a "fact" booklet with seemingly amiable guidelines that happen to be false.

At any rate, no large numbers of affected people appear to be diverted much from the main reality—that parole boards, like judges and prison officials, for the most part neglect altogether to supply information or explanations. With the federal board, this seems to be an article of positive pride. Describing itself and its functions in another official booklet, the board has written:

> . . . Voting is done on an individual basis by each member and the Board does not sit as a group for this purpose. Each member studies the prisoner's file and places his name on the official order form to signify whether he wishes to grant or deny parole. The reasoning and thought which led to his vote are not made a part of the order, and it is therefore impossible to state precisely why a particular prisoner was or was not granted parole.*

Not being positive whether the entire horror of that pronouncement comes home to a non-lawyer who is not devoted to Kafka, I labor what is probably patent. The parole board does not seem sheepish at all when it proclaims as doctrine that the reasons for its grave decisions are unknowable. In all disarming candor, it presents itself as the announced epitome of lawless authority. Its stance represents, moreover, a basic tenet of parole-board orthodoxy. Parole boards don't explain. They confer miracles or they refuse. For those refused, there is the signal of a downturned thumb and the comforting assurance that it has to be "impossible to state precisely why [he] . . . was not granted parole."

Of course, the impossibility is not God's will. Very recently, in what we may hope is a trail-blazing decision, the New Jersey Supreme Court ordered its state board to give reasons for a denial of parole.** The Federal Board of Parole begins to intimate some cognate changes of doctrine. The general fact remains, however, that most parole boards, subject to no precise rules of any kind, decree secretly and si-

* *Functions of the United States Board of Parole* pp. 4–5 (Washington, D.C., 1964).

** *Monks* v. *New Jersey State Parole Bd.*, 58 N.J. 238, 277 A.2d 193 (1971).

lently how tens and hundreds of thousands of convict-years shall be passed.

People in prison and students outside react with solidly grounded sentiments of cynicism and rage. Secret decisions bear no credentials of care or legitimacy. The belief is widespread that "politics" and corruption pervade the granting and denial of parole. The theory of rehabilitative benefit from the striving for parole is dissolved in an acid certainty among the supposed beneficiaries that the task is to find the muscle or the stratagems for beating a rotten system.

I have lingered at possibly morbid length over the characteristic failure of those in power to explain or account—from the day of sentence to the expiration of parole. This pervasive quality of irresponsibility is perhaps the most vivid evidence of fundamental lawlessness. But it is, of course, only evidence—mostly a symptom—rather than the root of the disorder. The basic problem remains the unruliness, the absence of rational ordering, the unbridled power of the sentencers to be arbitrary and discriminatory. The chapters that follow explore some possible means, existing and proposed, for dealing with these fundamentals.

Part Two

PALLIATIVES, REMEDIES, AND DIRECTIONS OF HOPE

5

Assumptions and Limitations

WHAT I HAVE written to this point is largely in the nature of what lawyers would call cumulative testimony. This is certainly not the first time anyone has charged or confessed that our methods of fixing penalties for crime are in central respects barbaric. It is perhaps fair to say that trial judges have not been prominent, though they have been included, among those voicing such criticisms. And it is my hope that judges bearing witness to such things may serve a useful purpose.

It remains true that other critics, less committed to and identified with the unrocked boat, have been less gentle. Some have concluded that the builders of institutions so defective must have been vicious or incompetent, or both. They have urged that the legal profession has sufficiently demonstrated its insufficiency, and that the grave business of punishment or treatment for crime must be transferred to more nearly qualified professional hands.

Harry Elmer Barnes, a devoted student of the subject, was moved to passionate denunciation of most judges, lawyers, and their colleagues in the existing business of punishment.

In a book he dedicated to Clarence S. Darrow, whom he characterized as "Foremost American Opponent of Juristic Savagery," he wrote:

> The diagnosis and treatment of the criminal is a highly technical medical and sociological problem for which the lawyer is rarely any better fitted than a real estate agent or a plumber. We shall ultimately come to admit that society has been as unfortunate in handing over criminals to lawyers and judges in the past as it once was in entrusting medicine to shamans and astrologers, and surgery to barbers. A hundred years ago we allowed lawyers and judges to have the same control of the insane classes as they still exert over the criminal groups, but we now recognize that insanity is a highly diversified and complex medical problem which we entrust to properly trained experts in the field of neurology and psychiatry. We may hope that in another hundred years the treatment of the criminal will be equally thoroughly and willingly submitted to medical and sociological experts.*

Apart from its unflattering tone, the quoted passage—or, certainly, its ultimate recommendation—would probably win substantial approval from many members of the legal profession. Though it is thought that few people yield power gladly, and this seems generally to be the case with judges not less than others, the loss of the sentencing power would be for many judges wonderfully bearable. For all my unkind treatment of their occasional foibles, large numbers of trial judges appreciate fully the unmanageable character of the sentencing power, and the doubts and the sorrows of its exercise. Many have urged, therefore, that supposed experts from other disciplines should take over the field. Trial lawyers are even more readily persuadable. Defense counsel especially, afflicted with recurrent evidences of their impotence at the sentencing stage, would be willing in droves to leave the scene earlier.

* *The Story of Punishment* (Boston, Stratford Co., 1930), pp. 265–6.

While any change in sentencing practices is likely to be an improvement, I doubt that wholly removing the responsibility and the power from the jurisdiction of the legal profession would be either feasible or desirable. As to feasibility, there are problems of a broadly political, or, more deeply perhaps, of a cultural and emotional nature. It is the settled way of long millennia that the judgment, the sentence, be pronounced by the magistrate commissioned to give or apply the law. Though judging has ceased, happily, to parade as a divine or kingly role, it partakes still of some of the subrational qualities that trailed in the wake of the king as judge. I do not urge such thoughts as necessarily good, only somewhat true. Insofar as notions of the august and the solemn still attend judges, they account in some measure for the remarkable degree to which judicial decrees continue to command acceptance and obedience.

These observations may not jibe minutely with what we know of contemporary skepticism concerning the sanctity of judges. But public affairs are filled with similar inconsistencies. It is a fact that judges—and the whole of the law—have known days of better repute. But the tradition of respect for the judicial office remains a fact, too. It seems clear that much would be lost in the way of habitual acceptance and compliance if the rendering of judgment were transferred wholly from the judicial to some more clinical office.*

It is questionable, moreover, whether there are other professions genuinely more "expert" to whom the ultimate responsibility would be better assigned. There are problems in sentencing, to be sure, of appraising and attempting to predict human behavior, and these we tend as laymen to

* It does not follow that the function should remain exclusively for judges. In Chapter 7 I suggest the desirability of having the judges share the sentencing responsibility with other professionals who have pertinent and complementary kinds of wisdom. However that suggestion is viewed, it is not decisive in any way of the thought here advanced—i.e., as to the peculiar habit of acceptance of judicial decrees.

consider the domain of psychiatrists or psychologists. But there is also a tendency to overrate the centrality of such problems and, with deference to them, the extent of effective knowledge possessed by psychiatrists and psychologists. It is not ingratitude or unkindness, but simple realism, to recognize that the study of human behavior is still an infant project and that reliable prediction remains thus far a rare possibility.

In sum, there is not a strong case in the nature of their professional wisdom for giving the duty of sentencing to students of individual human behavior. The same is true, I think, for other helping professions: social workers, educators, sociologists, and others have valuable knowledge to contribute, but scarcely enough, and scarcely enough of a broadly decisive nature, to vindicate claims by any or all of them to the sentencing responsibility. To the extent that other professionals have pertinent wisdom, it should, obviously, be enlisted for the task. But there is no group outside the law with cogent grounds for assumption of the final authority.

And this brings me to the *positive* reasons for believing that the power should continue to reside, with whatever aids and restrictions, where long history has placed it. The point is not simply, or mainly, that other professions are inadequately qualified. Rather, for all the wretchedness of our performance to date, I think vital aspects of the sentencing function are peculiarly *legal,* and peculiarly within the special competence of people legally trained. Granting that psychiatrists and other professionals have much to contribute, the eventual judgments as to criminal responsibility and the penalties for offenses are squarely within the legal order. They are judgments that must turn in the end upon the weighing of values, interests, and choices in the everyday province of legal rather than psychiatric study.

If lawyers have not thought enough, or well enough, about them, it remains true that the vital questions in this area are legal. Or at least, if they are not legal, they do not fall neatly within any other domain of scholarship or professional endeavor. Questions as to the purposes of punishment have, naturally, engaged philosophers, and we would do well to consult more the disparate things the philosophers have taught. But the relevant field of everyday working operations is the law. Likewise, gauging the gravity of particular offenses, the behavior of the defendant after prosecution begins, and the relationships between offenses and offenders are all matters of appropriate concern for people trained and at work with law rather than other disciplines.

Above all, lawfulness is, or ought to be, the cherished and constant concern of the legal profession.* Our training and daily practice are in the fashioning, manipulating, and perfecting of law. Our business centers upon the creation of general and intelligible rules, the understanding of their limits, the techniques for their fair application, and the corollary dimensions of allowable discretion. The special discipline of the law ranges across every imaginable relationship and field of learning. It makes no decisive difference that the field to be regulated is economics or art or psychiatry. The antitrust counsel or the copyright specialist or the criminal lawyer may indeed require the guidance of economists or artists or psychiatrists. But the law job is in the end the lawyer's. And that, I submit, is the way sentencing must be viewed during at least the foreseeable future.

The profound defects in the handling of sentencing are by no means the inevitable consequences of legal management. Quite to the contrary, the main evils assailed by me (among many others) reflect largely the absence of decent

* Ambrose Bierce supplied a more cynical formulation, which is worth recalling for fun and, possibly, for the useful dash of acid balance the cynic supplies. His definition of "lawful" in *The Devil's Dictionary* (American Century Series, New York, Hill and Wang), p. 103 (1961) is:

> Compatible with the will of a judge having jurisdiction.

legal ordering. The absurdly broad statutes, the gross inequalities, the unchecked discretion of judges, the absence of reasoned explanations, the haste and the general arbitrariness—all are defects the legal profession is schooled to identify and remedy, not really to foster. The problem has been too little law, not too much.

In proceeding, then, to consider possible roads to improvement, I start with the assumption that sentencing not only will be, but probably should be, left in the hands of judges, with lawyers participating in some variants of their existing roles. As should be apparent already, this does not mean at all that the judges should go on as they have been, that they may be expected themselves to cure the existing disorders, or that others should not have enlarged shares of responsibility. It does mean that if my combined forecast and preference are wrong, corollary errors are likely to appear in the views expressed below.

Having warned of that, let me make some further disclosures and disclaimers that may explain or supply perspective for the following chapters. My basic premises about sentencing include a firm conviction that we in this country send far too many people to prison for terms that are far too long. Depending on classification schemes, the rankings may vary somewhat, but the United States probably has the longest sentences by a wide margin of any industrialized nation.* It is my belief that prison terms ought on the whole

* A distinguished study and report from an American Bar Association group said this in 1967:

> While comparative statistics are always subject to many interpretations and qualifications, it is nevertheless instructive to examine the practice in other countries, if only superficially. In England, for example, sentences in the range of twenty to thirty years "are now entirely exceptional . . . and are generally disapproved." . . . Sentences in excess of five years are rare in most European countries. . . . In 1964 in Sweden there were only eight commitments out of 11,227 to a term of more than ten years, and only thirty-eight to a term exceeding four years. There were in addition

to be much shorter. Also, that some considerable percentage of those we send to prison ought not to be so confined. This means that alternatives to prisons—for example, probation, work release, halfway houses, fines—must be employed more, and that creative thought must be devoted to expanding and improving the varieties of alternatives.

These points, ticked off so quickly here, go plainly to fundamentals. I mention them in part to reveal debatable preferences. In addition, I would hope that the failure to dwell upon matters of such consequence will not be read as slighting their importance. The subjects I have seen fit to explore in this small book are in a broad sense procedural. They have to do with essentially two categories: *first,* the apparatus—the personnel, their relationships, and the character of the rules governing them—for sentencing; and *second,* the organization of research, study, and lawmaking for the ongoing business of reform. These subjects, if not the most romantic, are in my view prime and fundamental. I am afflicted, understandably perhaps, with a lawyer's conviction that fair and effective procedures are, if not life's blood itself, its vital circulatory system.* I think the ultimate questions of substance—the length, frequency, and kinds of sentences—will not be handled with rationality and overall fairness until we have organized the work of evolving rational and fair principles of law. Similarly, I think the evils of excessive power will not be cured by the appearance of superhuman officials, but by following the teachings of the

692 indeterminate commitments which in practice tend to result in release after an average of five years.

A.B.A. Project on Minimum Standards for Criminal Justice, Standards Relating to Sentencing Alternatives and Procedures, approved by the A.B.A. House of Delegates in August 1968, (New York, Office of Criminal Justice Project, 1968), p. 57.

* "The history of liberty has largely been the history of observance of procedural safeguards." Mr. Justice Frankfurter, in *McNabb* v. *United States,* 318 U.S. 332, 347 (1943).

Founding Fathers and fashioning controls over fallible men and women. With these as basic premises, my ultimate proposals are means for producing reforms rather than a closed catalogue of definitive changes.

Before tendering those proposals, however, it is essential to recognize that we do not write on a clean slate. Long years of discontent have produced at least some devices and arrangements for the pursuit of rationality in sentencing. The chapters immediately following this one describe existing ideas for the improvement of judges (Chapter 6), the sharing of the powers now exercised by the single trial judge and provisions for review of sentencing decisions (Chapter 7), and the divestiture of the judges' powers by transfers to parole boards or similar agencies (Chapter 8). After considering such things, their limits and their potential, I conclude (in Chapter 9) with an outline of my own tentative ideas both for some immediate reforms and for a longer-range program of study and change.

6

Sentencing Institutes

IT IS WIDELY known, if not generally trumpeted from the courthouses, that judges are both variable and imperfect. Since sentences for crime reflect both of these qualities—namely, in the disparities and the perversities of sentences—it has been thought on occasion that substantial improvements could be wrought by improving the judges. Responsive to the perceived difficulties, the ideas tend to center upon two modes of possible enlightenment: *one,* to have the judges exchange—and thus, it is hoped, to harmonize—their views; *second,* to have the judges educated by "experts." Both conceptions underlie the relatively modern device known as the "sentencing institute."

By a law passed in 1958, Congress provided for the periodic convening of sentencing institutes. The proposal had come from the federal judges themselves, through the Judicial Conference of the United States.* The impetus, as a House re-

* The Judicial Conference consists of the Chief Justice as head, the Chief Judges of the Eleven Circuits, and representatives of other federal courts. It studies problems of administering justice and makes reports and recommendations to Congress and the courts.

port described it, was concern about "widespread disparities in the sentences imposed by Federal courts . . . in different parts of the country, between adjoining districts, and even in the same districts." * The institutes are intended under the statute to bring together, from time to time, judges, United States Attorneys, and others from the Department of Justice, "specialists in sentencing methods, criminologists, psychiatrists, penologists, and others to participate in the proceedings.** Such convocations are designed, the law says, to promote "the interest of uniformity in sentencing procedures" by "studying, discussing, and formulating the objectives, policies, standards, and criteria for sentencing those convicted of crimes and offenses in the courts of the United States." † The Congress is not a philosophers' grove, so nobody paused in the passage of the act over the revelation that in 1958 we were just getting around to an arrangement for "formulating the objectives, policies, standards, and criteria for sentencing. . . ."

However late that might have seemed if anyone had thought about it, the idea had a goodly sound. Many of us reacted with the kind of unstinting gratification often exhibited when a virtuous resolution is experienced as the achievement of virtue. The Deputy Attorney General, who was a former district judge and highly successful lawyer, told the assemblage at the first sentencing institute that the new program was "important because it reconciles the need for judicial independence with the need for consistency." ‡ He did not labor the point; he avoided the tedium of explaining how the new institutes would achieve so wondrous a reconciliation. But he did what lawyers frequently do when

* H.R. Rep. No. 1946, 85th Cong., 2d Sess., p. 6 (1958).

** 28 U.S.C. §334(c).

† *Ibid.*, subsection (a).

‡ Lawrence E. Walsh, "An Expression of Interest on the Part of the Department of Justice," Pilot Institute on Sentencing, 26 F. R. D. 250 (1959).

they find it necessary to omit (usually because they lack) documentation: he repeated and praised the unexplained conclusion. He predicted that the "institutes should influence the judiciary toward consistency without regimentation of any sort." * He gave the judges a superfluous reminder of how splendid they were and how unseemly it would be to hobble them with the kinds of "rules and regulations needed to control large numbers of people. . . ." His words, not because I agree with them, merit somewhat fuller quotation. The new program of institutes, he said,

> takes into account the fact that judges are not produced in mass quantity, and that rules and regulations of a kind needed to control large numbers of people are inappropriate with regard to the Federal judiciary. Each Federal judge has been selected with a great deal of care and pride by some administration and by his own Bar. The need for rigidity is not present here. In fact, to get the most out of the qualities that a judge brings to his country's service, the absence of rigidity is required. Yet the exchange of views is necessary, and these institutes lend themselves so ideally to this.**

Other speakers hailed the institution of the institutes with similar sounds of congratulation and self-congratulation.

As is often true, however, the enthusiasms of the inaugural addresses found only the thinnest echoes in the administration of the program. Sentencing institutes, as was fairly foreseeable, appear to have been trivial and sometime things. In accordance with the statute, the judges from a single federal circuit, occasionally two or more circuits,† do meet

* *Ibid.*

** *Ibid.*, pp. 250–1.

† For laymen it may not hurt to mention that the country is divided into just under one hundred districts and eleven circuits for federal-court purposes. Each district (sometimes a district is an entire state, as are, say, Utah and New Jersey; sometimes a state is divided into several districts, as, for example, Alabama and California) has a district court as its trial court or, more compendiously, "court of first instance." Above the district

now and then in sentencing institutes. The institutes do commonly include non-judicial participants—probation officers, parole officials, prosecutors, private lawyers, even an occasional scholar—who often take leadership or teaching roles. The institutes run for a day or two. The topics covered may include sentencing in particular kinds of cases (tax fraud, auto theft, selective-service violations, etc.), general information on sentencing alternatives (the setting of parole eligibility, commitments for study, etc.), and, occasionally, some ideas about possible reforms of the law. Probably the most frequent type of session, and that most congenial to lawyers trained in our common-law tradition of concentration upon concrete cases, is the discussion of specific sentencing situations and the various ways the participants have handled, or would handle, them. In this typical activity, actual presentence reports are duplicated and distributed; the judges study them individually; then they meet to state and discuss their individual views. To nobody's surprise, the judges exhibit huge divergences in their dispositions of the same case. Everybody tends to gasp a little upon the rehearing of this old story. Sometimes, but not regularly, a judge seems to be persuaded toward some view different from his initial one. But there is no binding "decision" on anything. The kaleidoscopic independences of the judges remain intact. They leave about as miscellaneous and unpredictable as they were when they arrived.

The institutes are undoubtedly of some utility. But their

courts is the court of appeals for each circuit, with each circuit (except the District of Columbia) embracing several states—as, for example, the First Circuit, covering Maine, Massachusetts, New Hampshire, Rhode Island, and, perhaps quaintly, Puerto Rico. At the top, of course, above the courts of appeals, is the Supreme Court. There are also a number of specialized federal courts—the Tax Court, Court of Claims, Customs Court, Court of Customs and Patent Appeals, and Court of Military Appeals. Except for the last, these specialized courts are not concerned usually or directly with problems of crime and punishment.

worth could easily be overstated. They serve to remind older judges, and perhaps to inform new judges, of sentencing options that might otherwise be overlooked. They supply rare occasions for judges to face each other and try out with their peers such organized premises and attitudes as they may have touching the business of sentencing. For those who do not genuinely think connected thoughts about the subject, the institutes may instigate at least a temporary disposition to reflect.

While that much is worthwhile, it is a small record of achievement after all. And it is difficult to conceive how anyone could truly have anticipated more from brief, infrequent, and sketchily organized conclaves of this nature. As to the infrequency, without certifying it as absolutely typical, I think my own experience is probably not utterly atypical. In what is, at this writing, a total of some seven years on the largest of the federal district courts, I have spent two afternoons at sentencing institutes, one within my own circuit, the other at a national seminar for "new" judges, to which I was invited after two and one-half years on the bench and some hundreds of years of prison sentences imposed. This may be below average for federal judges. It is unlikely to be sufficiently below to affect the basic point that the institutes cannot have major impact on judicial thought and functioning.

As I have indicated, the subjects treated at the institutes have a somewhat random, partial, and almost accidental quality. And the results are determinedly inconclusive. There may be a "consensus" about some subjects—meaning, most or many of the judges agree on some general propositions. Most or many may agree, to repeat a favorite example of mine, that a defendant merits consideration for pleading guilty rather than standing trial. This entails necessarily, however, that at least a few, or some substantial number, take a different or opposite view—e.g., that giving a guilty plea weight in a defendant's favor has the effect of penalizing people who exercise their basic right to a trial with the presumption of innocence. The discovery of consensuses or majority views may interest scholars. It does not cure the essential evil of disparity—that the sentence a man receives depends on the accident of what judge has been assigned his case. Perhaps a "cure" is a lot to ask. In the statute providing for sentencing institutes, Congress set as a goal "a desirable degree of consensus" among the judges. Something is surely accomplished if there is a tendency toward equality notwithstanding the failure to achieve equal treatment. But the actual benefit even in these terms seems paltry. Whatever "desirable" means, the evidence of reported "consensus" has not been impressive. Besides, it does not appear that the institutes can themselves be credited with the actual promotion, as distinguished from the reporting, of consensus. And, above all, "consensus"—an approach to agreement that roughly similar legal consequences will follow most of the time from roughly similar conduct—is not thought commonly to define the ideal of a system of *law*.

For the furtherance of this ideal in sentencing, the device of the sentencing institute is almost entirely irrelevant. The requirement of objective rules, equally applied, is not supposed, after all, to be served by having judges counsel together or take courses. Overstating the point only a little, we do not rely for fair application of our tax or tort or contract laws upon "institutes" in which the judges compare notes and find out how much (or little) they may agree with each other on who should pay how much for some particular kind of conduct. How much anyone "pays" normally is a consequence of applying *law* to the particular set of facts. Identical facts are to produce identical consequences. (To be sure, that beguiling simplicity raises a host of problems beyond our subject, but nobody doubts it as a fair statement of a basic goal.) We don't seek a "desirable degree" of known and uniform law through institutes. We mandate it through the organs of government empowered to declare the law.

If I am correct, then, in believing that the basic evil is an absence of adequate law, seminars and institutes about sentencing function in a vacuum. There is not enough to teach or to discuss meaningfully. Some useful things are undoubtedly possible. Given a setting of general ignorance and uncertainty, it is still possible for judges to acquire some guidelines and some wisdom over time. It follows that exchanges of learning and experience are not wholly useless. The earnest judges, by no means rare, may grow through shared experience and thought in poise, grace, sympathy, understanding, and fortitude. What they cannot do is make laws of fair and equal application in institutes which are chartered to reconcile "the need for judicial independence with the need for consistency."

This is a good point for stopping and taking some swings at the notion of "judicial independence," which plays a perverse and misbegotten role in discussions of sentencing. Every thoughtful citizen of a democracy wants an independent judiciary. What we mean, however, or ought to mean, is a body of judges protected by tradition and institutional safeguards against non-legal, unruly, arbitrary pressures weighting the scales of justice on one side or the other. So, for example, judges are to be sheltered from the clamor of the mob and from immediate punishment or reward for their decisions. I refer here to "immediate" consequences, avoiding a debate that would take us too far afield. But the reader is reminded in passing that our federal Constitution (like the laws of only two or three states) guards the judge against even more remote influences by providing for life tenure (at least "during good behavior," which may be disproved only in rare and difficult impeachment proceedings). Similarly, the Federal Constitution forbids reduction of judges' salaries "during their continuance in office." And we have a host of other safeguards for "independence," closely allied as it is with the quintessential attribute of impartiality.

But the vital concept, like many in the law and elsewhere, is capable of running amok as an untethered abstraction, especially when this is sensed, consciously or not, to be convenient. Nobody means by "judicial independence" that judges ought to be unrestrained by binding rules of law. Yet that is in essence what is meant when people say the sentencing judge should be "influenced toward consistency" but "without regimentation of any sort." In this sense, the idea of independence is, of course, distorted and pernicious, not to say silly. I think the misconception has played a large role in clouding vision concerning needed reform of our sentencing system. Thus, I plan to reiterate this denunciation when we come in the next chapter to the subjects of multi-judge sentencing and appeals from sentences. Similarly, to recall the fundamental evil already canvassed, "judicial independence" has often been thought to justify the unpredictability and inequality of sentences, even though no one trained in law would accept a decisional crazy quilt of this kind for other subjects.

To end this essentially thin topic, the education of judges in sentencing institutes or other conclaves is not a promising route to fundamental improvements. The idea ought not to be scrapped. Indeed, as an adjunct of more profound reforms, it may evolve into a meaningful kind of effort. For the crying needs, however, other, better, more intensive, and more aptly focused enterprises are needed.

7

Limiting Trial Judges

IT IS FAR from a novelty to contend, as I do, that the sweeping power of a single judge to determine the sentence, as a matter of largely unreviewable "discretion," is a—perhaps "the"—central evil in the system. No long leap of the imagination is required to move from that perception to the formulation of at least two species of reform proposals: (1) have the single judge "checked and balanced" by sharing his power; (2) have his sentencing decisions subject to appellate review, as are most of the ultimate rulings (mostly far less important) of our trial judges. While ideas of this kind are not mysterious, and while they are widely extant, the degree of their acceptance and implementation in our country has been remarkably scant. I plan to discuss three such measures, their fate thus far, and the issues generated by them.

SENTENCING COUNCILS

Beginning a dozen or so years ago, the judges of the United States District Court for the Eastern District of Michigan (Detroit) began to meet weekly to share their worries about sentences. By and by, their sessions came to be regularized and somewhat formalized, and were dubbed "sentencing councils." The Detroit judges proceeded soon to share their experience in talks and legal periodicals. Their proselytizing efforts led to adoption of the practice in two other Federal Districts, the Eastern District of New York (Brooklyn, Long Island, Staten Island) and the Northern District of Illinois (Chicago). There, to this writing, the spread has stopped. Before commenting on that, let me describe the procedure very briefly and render it some deserved praise.

In broad outline, the arrangement is that not only the judge who is charged with the particular case but two of his fellow judges as well will receive copies of the presentence report. Each of the three studies the report and notes the tentative sentence he might base upon that reading alone. The three then meet, usually with a probation officer in attendance, compare their preliminary estimates, and discuss the case. Upon the basis of that session, the judge responsible for the case may or may not, as a matter of his exclusive judgment, revise his own initial appraisal. That judge then presides in the usual way at the sentencing hearing, imposing the sentence his judgment finally dictates, which may duplicate his earliest thought, a consensus with his colleagues, or neither of these. The actual sentence is then reported to the others and recorded for possible further discussion and, of course, for retrospective study.

The experience of the courts employing this device has been ample enough by now to supply some interesting, if not startling, conclusions: (1) The sentencing judge appears in a substantial percentage of cases to move from his own tentative stance toward an ultimate sentence reflecting in some measure the views of his fellow judges. (2) The individual extremes of sentencing inclination, both harsh and lenient, tend to be tempered. The tough judges appear to grow gentler, the milder ones seem to become sterner. (3) While there is that tendency toward a mean, the net effect overall seems to be toward lenity; taken all together, the participating judges give shorter prison terms and make increased use of probation rather than confinement.

As I have indicated, the judges working with the sentencing-council device are pleased with it, and they have proclaimed its virtues to their colleagues elsewhere. As I have also mentioned, the practice has not spread like wildfire. It is interesting, in a somewhat disheartening way, to consider why not.

Perhaps the main obstacle to the wider use of sentencing councils is the reluctance of judges to invest the added time for considering their colleagues' cases and for meetings. One need not be hostile to judges or to their interest in self-preservation to find this a trivial concern when it is measured against the end in view. A time-and-motion study would reveal that every trial judge spends countless hours on minutiae that cannot compare in significance with the effort to formulate wise and reasoned sentences. Varying with the court, all of us have listened to extensive evidence and brooded at length about the damage award for a shipment of defective hosiery, the claim that one dull fabric design was copied from another dull fabric design, questions of "fault" in auto-accident cases, etc. I do not mean to deprecate unduly the importance of such concerns or the deep interest they hold for the litigants. It is enough to say that sentencing matters more. If there are not judge-hours enough to improve this vital enterprise, we should cut out other things, add judges, work harder, or do some of each.

A second argument heard repeatedly against the sentencing council is that it is a threat or an affront to the "independence" of the sentencing judge. I have sought in the preceding chapter to expose and correct this fallacious conception of independence. Here, I would add only that the worry is quite clearly beside the point in any event. The proponents of sentencing councils, perhaps to exorcise this goblin, have emphasized steadily that the presiding judge retains unfettered power to determine the sentence. It is surely a pathological "independence" that needs or deserves protection against the impact of discussion, criticism, and possibly variant ideas. This is not to concede that the unchecked power of the single judge is desirable to begin with. One of my central themes is, of course, to the contrary. But assuming such power ought to exist, the sentencing council in no way impairs it. It will cause at worst a more thoughtful and informed exercise of the power.

There is, finally, an argument heard less frequently. This is the point that the sentencing council is unfair to the defendant because it allows the decision as to sentence to be made, or at least influenced, by people he has no opportunity to confront directly. The argument has surface appeal, but no more. Again, of course, it is relevant that the single trial judge retains unimpaired his control over the sentence, and the defendant confronts and may address that judge on the day of sentence. (I have mentioned earlier how empty a ritual this is in most cases.) Beyond that, it is a mistake to suppose that under the standard procedure, nobody may influence outside the courtroom the course of the sentencing decision. Judges regularly confer with probation officers. Nothing prohibits informal consultations with fellow judges, though, concededly, these seem to be infrequent. It is unacceptable generally in our system that *evidence* be obtained ex parte, without giving affected parties an opportunity to meet it or know it is being used. This is the core idea in the so-called "right of confrontation"—the right of the accused, as the Sixth Amendment to our Constitution states it, "to be confronted with the witnesses against him." But that sensible protection has never been supposed—and nobody has ever tried to make it serve—to insulate the judge from judgmental considerations, ideas of value, policy, and fairness. Such ideas infiltrate from books, colleagues, perhaps people generally. The technique of consultation to air and explore the relevant facets of the complex sentencing problem is not, and should not be, either forbidden or avoided on the supposed ground of prejudice to the defendant.

It is my belief, in sum, that the sentencing council is superior to the orthodox technique of decision by a single judge consulting no others. The council does not by itself affect the things I have identified as root problems—the absence of precise rules and the corollary excess of discretion left to the deciders. But it would, I think, represent a distinct improvement if nothing further or different were done by way of reform.*

What is more striking than any such individual view is the fact that each multi-judge federal court has been left free—"independent"—to decide for itself whether to use sentencing councils. It is not claimed that eleven or twelve years of experimentation in three busy courts have supplied insufficient basis for judgment. We have here simply another illustration of the anomalous notion that judges should be left to do much as they please with respect to sentencing. I repeat my most basic objection: that such unfettered variations are intolerable in a rational system of *law*. There are bedrock principles with us for the making of law and its general application. The decision on whether to use sentencing councils ought to be made a matter of law, applicable alike to all objectively similar situations. If the councils are in that way determined to be desirable, they should be required wherever the personnel and facilities for their

* The fact that sentencing councils are not used in my own court is only one among many illustrations that a majority of our judges (now an authorized complement of twenty-seven) does not always share my perceptions of truth and beauty.

employment exist. There is no justification for local option in fundamentals of this nature.

MIXED SENTENCING TRIBUNALS

Over thirty-five years ago, Professor Sheldon Glueck, the noted Harvard criminologist, wrote persuasively that sentencing is too important and difficult to be left to judges alone. Elaborating an idea others had sketched before, he proposed that sentences be assessed by a panel of three: (1) the judge, (2) a psychiatrist or psychologist, and (3) a sociologist or educator.* The suggestion has not been adopted anywhere. Yet its essential soundness seems evident. Nobody who thinks can believe that judges are expert in the many things relevant to sentencing. It is clear that the knowledge of psychiatrists and other groups like those Glueck suggested is relevant. Scraps of data from their domains are given to the sentencing judge in presentence reports, and perhaps understood in some degree by him. But scarcely with the deep or rounded understanding of experts.

There is more to this than the addition of new varieties of technical expertise narrowly understood. People with such other backgrounds as those Glueck would import think differently, and view the world differently, than do the generality of judges. There are overlaps and exceptions, but it seems safe to say as a general matter that such things as youthful behavior (or misbehavior), propensities to violence, drug addiction, and sexual misconduct are likely to present varying qualities and evoke varying responses from members of the several professions. Insofar as the world's phenomena are to be dealt with in strictly "legal" terms, if that is ever literally possible, it is fitting that they be left exclusively to lawyers and judges. But criminal sentences, at least as now conceived, are not so confined. The insights of others

* *Crime and Justice* (Boston, Little, Brown and Co., 1936), pp. 225–6.

who study human behavior are obviously germane to the rendition of such judgments.

Of course, if sentencing councils are seen as incompatible with judicial independence, Glueck's proposal is unspeakable. Moreover, the mixed tribunal would present difficult problems of support and administration. Without pursuing such complexities, I have no doubt they could all be managed if the idea were deemed desirable. But the realistic prospects seem no less bleak than they were in 1936. Having been led to focus mainly in another quarter, I leave Professor Glueck's proposition barely recalled, tarrying only to regret the casual neglect it has thus far enjoyed.

APPELLATE REVIEW OF SENTENCING

Our system of justice, civil as well as criminal, is not notably speedy. To many of those who worry about law and order, the concern is that punishment for crime should be more certain, more severe, and, not least of all, swifter. Without stopping over the intricacies and varieties of views about "law and order," most of us may wonder from time to time whether appellate scrutiny of the criminal process does not tend in some respects to be excessively lengthy, detailed, and minute. Appellate courts write annual volumes about pretrial procedure, arrests, searches, phrases spoken to juries, rulings on evidence, and other episodes in or around the trial level. The ultimate goal, for all its imperfections, is precious. We strive to perfect and safeguard the grim process of detecting crime and ascertaining the truth about criminal charges. We are, at least most of us—usually—willing to pay a large price in time and "inefficiency" because personal security and *liberty* are at stake.

On a wide scale, however, the concern ends at the point of measuring the loss of liberty for the criminal defendant. In the federal courts and in some two-thirds of the states, there is in practical effect *no appeal* from the trial judge's sentence. To be slightly technical—i.e., accurate—I mean that a sentence within the prescribed maximum limits cannot be lowered on appeal. There are no genuine "exceptions" to this, though there are rare and narrow occasions when a higher court will correct or set aside the sentence as such. Thus, for example, if a trial judge were shown to have given a severe sentence on grounds of race or religion, his action could not stand. But this would not be because of "excessiveness." It would be because the impermissible (unconstitutional) criterion would fatally infect the judgment and destroy its allowable character as an exercise of judicial discretion. There are other cases of similar kind and similar infrequency.*

The basic point remains as I have stated it: neither the federal courts nor most states provide for any effective appellate review of sentences. I cannot know whether the reader finds this as horrendous as I do after living with it as a fact of professional life for many years. Consider that a civil judgment for $2,000 is reviewable in every state at least once,

* The legal theory of this passage is familiar to lawyers, but may warrant a word of elaboration for laymen. Broadly speaking, a sentencing judge has discretion up to the statutory maximum and cannot be reversed if he stays within that maximum. But he is deemed not to be exercising lawful discretion at all if he allows himself to be moved by outrageous and legally excluded considerations such as skin color or religion of the defendant. Then his judgment must be nullified and the defendant must be re-sentenced in accordance with law.

But would you ever know that the judge transgressed the wide limits of his discretion by allowing race prejudice or the like to affect his decision? Hardly. I know of no specific case where such an atrocity is specifically disclosed, although the statistical evidence of its existence is strong. On the other hand, there are rare cases of judicial errors similar in legal theory if not in degree of horror. So, for example, judges have said on the record that (as other judges believe but do not announce) they give *all* draft evaders long prison terms instead of considering for each defendant the range from zero to five years. Such mechanical uniformity is a failure to exercise discretion and is, therefore, reversible error. Another case of analogous character is mentioned above, on pp. 41–2.

possibly on two appellate levels. Then consider the unreviewability of a sentence of twenty years in prison and a fine of $10,000. Consider that a distinguished committee of the American Bar Association, not normally an agency of revolution, when it urged appellate review of sentences in a report adopted and endorsed by the association in 1968, pointed out "that in no other area of our law does one man exercise such unrestricted power [as the trial judge's unreviewable sentencing power]. No other country in the free world permits this condition to exist." *

There are many reasons for this dubious distinction, none sufficient in my view. Before tearing at them, I report from random (and unscientific) samplings over a number of years the observation that most judges, both trial and appellate, seem satisfied with the status quo in this respect not less than others. There is no single position, naturally. But most trial judges, for all their protests about the agonies of the ultimate responsibility for sentencing, oppose the idea of appellate review. I shall come to the commonly *stated* reasons. First, if cynically, I suggest that one substantial reason, not commonly stated, is the (recognizably human) aversion to being criticized and countermanded. Most trial judges seek to follow, within their capacities, what they perceive as the controlling views of higher courts. It is a consistent, if not an inescapable, corollary that many at least are not keen to expand the scope of such controls. It is equally clear that this reluctance by itself is no valid reason for barring appellate review of sentences.

On this subject, appellate judges, if normally viewed as natural enemies, are numerously allied with the trial bench. Lending the most august support is Chief Justice Warren E.

* A.B.A. Project on Minimum Standards for Criminal Justice, *Standards Relating to Appellate Review of Sentences*, approved by the A.B.A. House of Delegates in February 1968, New York, Office of Criminal Justice Project, 1968, pp. 1–2.

Burger, who has voiced more than once his opposition to appellate review of sentences, at least if conducted by the standard appellate tribunals.* Again, the ranks are not closed; for example, Senior Judge Simon E. Sobeloff, former Chief of the Fourth Circuit (embracing Virginia, West Virginia, North and South Carolina), has long argued for review of sentences, lately adding to his writings and talks his service as head of the valuable A.B.A. Advisory Committee mentioned a few pages ago.

As is true of the trial judges, those on appellate courts have varying reasons, of varying cogency, for opposing review. One is the volume of new work it would entail. This, if better than the concern of trial judges not to be reversed more than they already are, is not enough better to warrant much discussion. Considering all the things on which appellate judges ponder, the effort to make sentences more rational and just would hardly seem unworthy of their labors.

It is also argued, with somewhat greater substance, that the review of sentences might distort the appellate process. In slightly inflated and cloudy terms, the thought has been put this way:

> . . . Appellate courts are designed to be students of the law, to consider questions of the law, and to act in a dispassionate and detached atmosphere. If there were to be appellate review, proceedings in appellate courts would be corrupted by appeals to emotion and sympathy, and the other things that go into sentence. As a result these great institutions would be deteriorated.**

* The Chief Justice has spoken in favor of a form of review by a panel of trial judges. Provisions for such review exist in four states. With all deference, I doubt the desirability of such a procedure. Judges of the same level reviewing each other have inhibitions and discomforts that impair the effectiveness of the appeal. Besides, for reasons touched on below, there are good grounds for having the appeal on the sentence combined with other questions raised for review.

** Lawrence E. Walsh, *op. cit.*, p. 251.

A closely related argument is that making sentences reviewable might lead appellate judges to bargain in the disposition of appeals, trading off votes for affirmance against votes to reduce sentence.

This whole pattern of interrelated ideas serves to highlight the horrors of our attitudes on sentencing, not to sustain rationally the position against appealability. The notion that sentencing involves "emotion and sympathy," and thus could pollute the appellate process, reverberates with disturbing implications. If the thought has validity, what qualifies our trial judges to be trusted with this responsibility? Are matters of emotion and sympathy uncheckable—unreviewable? Are appellate judges really free in their daily work from emotion and sympathy? Among the answers to these questions is the vital point that the power to send people to prison for long stretches ought to be exercised in a system of law on grounds more objective and rational than vague sentiment. Insofar as decisions of this kind are likely to involve feeling as well as intellection, this is a factor adding to the need for a second look by the relatively detached appellate tribunals. If emotion and sympathy are inevitable factors, it would not really hurt appellate judges to suffer these qualities of the human experience. What is more to the point is that the virtues of a higher court include its separation from the face-to-face forensics of the trial court, promoting a useful quality of cool objectivity, even about matters that generate intense feeling in their immediate occurrence.

The fear that sentence review would lead to (presumably improper) bargaining in the appellate court has its own train of interesting premises. The basic assumption here is, of course, that there is and should be a rigorous separation between (1) the question of guilt or innocence, or, more strictly speaking, the validity of the conviction, and (2) the propriety of the sentence. It is certainly true that we act upon this assumption in a number of respects. It is also true, however, that the conceptual separation is not inescapably sound in principle and not uniformly enforceable in practice.

It is standard in the federal courts and most state trials to instruct juries that they are to concentrate exclusively on guilt or innocence, leaving the question of punishment, if there is a conviction, for the trial judge.* This embodies vividly the idea of separateness of the two determinations. It reflects, to acknowledge the reach of the idea, that error must follow from "confusing" the questions (1) "did the defendant do it?" with (2) "if he did, what may or should be the penalty?" It is not the least bit doubtful that the questions are distinct and that the answer to one ought not logically to be influenced by the answer to the other. But when we descend to the slovenly real world of illogic and uncertainty, the neatness of the categories becomes blurred. Verdicts rest upon probabilities, not absolute certainties. To minimize ghastly mistakes, we demand a high probability for criminal conviction. We require proof that is "beyond a reasonable doubt." While the quoted words state the standard in *all* criminal cases, it seems unlikely as a practical matter that they always mean the same thing. It is questionable that a "reasonable doubt" in a case involving a hundred-dollar fine is the same kind or degree of reservation as it is in a case involving imprisonment for a long term of years. I suggest, however unorthodox it may sound, that the meaning *should not* be identical: we ought to be more sure of our ground in the graver case than in the relatively minor one.

There are instances in which the illogical intertwining of the verdict as to guilt with ideas about the sentence is less readily defensible in principle, but compellingly understand-

* Among the exceptions to this has been the procedure in some states for jury recommendations or decisions on capital punishment. In addition, a dozen or more states give to juries the authority to set terms of imprisonment.

able in terms of basic human values. It is recorded, for example, that in eighteenth-century England, when scores of crimes, including many we now deem petty, were punishable by death,* juries mitigated the horror by simply refusing on a large scale to convict, notwithstanding clear demonstrations of "guilt." If that could be shunted aside as laymen's irresponsibility, we know of similar conduct by the professionals not similarly discountable. There is solid evidence in our own day that trial judges sitting without juries in cases involving stiff mandatory minimum sentences (e.g., *not less than* five years or more than twenty) have acquitted defendants they believed guilty because they deemed the minimum sentence outlandishly high for the particular case. That is a questionable course for a judge to follow. I do not linger to defend it. I merely mention it as a possibly relevant, interesting fact of legal life.

The upshot of the last few paragraphs is that the sharp division between questions as to guilt and questions as to sentence (1) is not always, and (2) should not always be, maintained. The fear that appellate judges will "confuse" the two subjects is overdrawn even in legal theory. Moreover, there are times when the two should by rights be thought about together. In a close case with a huge sentence, it makes sense to consider reduction of sentence as a possibly preferable alternative to outright reversal of the conviction. Insofar as the two subjects should be sealed off from each other, we must either rely upon our appellate judges to do right, or acknowledge that we are engaged in a comedy of straining at gnats.

It is relevant to note that our rule of non-appealability of sentences is maintained at some uncertain cost in hypocrisy and evasion. Deferring to the rule, appellate judges, being at least somewhat subject to "emotion and sympathy," are

* Including, for example, forgery, sheep-stealing, the picking of pockets, and threats to burn a barn or hayloft.

periodically horrified by cases in which the sentences, though within maximum limits, seem cruelly excessive in the circumstances. The most common response is a sorrowful wringing of hands, some wistful observations, and a futile reaffirmation of the appellate court's powerlessness to right the evident wrong. Not infrequently, however, the appellate judges will search out some strained species of "error" in the trial, not because they genuinely deem it a proper ground for reversal, but as a pretext for setting aside the intolerable sentence. Sometimes the appeals court will slip into the inelegant role of supplicant before the trial judge. Confessing impotence to review the sentence and finding no plausible ground for reversal, the appellate opinion will suggest that the sentence seems, perhaps, a bit barbarous and would the trial judge perhaps, when the case comes back to him, please be willing to have another look.

None of the several dodges or stratagems is seemly. A candid rule of appealability of sentences is plainly to be preferred. If the view persists that questions about sentence ought to be sharply separated from other questions, the obvious implementation is to have a separate appeal concerned exclusively with the sentence. This is the practice in England, where there is a distinct and separate "appeal against sentence." My own view is that one compendious appeal ought to deal with everything on which review is sought. But this is a relatively small detail. The main thing is to have *some* system of open, thorough, straightforward review on appeal of the sentencing decision.

One substantial issue remains to be mentioned. It is said often that sentencing is a matter of "discretion," as distinguished from "law," and hence is unsuited for inclusion among the "questions of law" that comprise the domain of appellate courts. Interwoven with this theme is the conventional assertion that the trial judge has the unique and unreproducible advantages of seeing the defendant, "sizing him up" and possessing from daily exposure a seasoned wisdom in the use of such firsthand impressions. Appellate judges studying a "cold record" are in this light unable to contribute, but will only impair the sentencing process with their second guesses.

Disposing first of the latter point, I think it fair to describe it as minor and largely phony. The trial judge's keen eyes and ears have been mythologized in more contexts than this one. The uses of the trial and the sentencing hearing for appraising the defendant in relevant respects are much overrated. The trial judge's powers of effective observation are likewise exaggerated; some judges are astute people-watchers and may sometimes learn useful things. But the whole subject is overblown, and the conclusion against appellate review does not follow in any event. It is familiar in the law that an appellate court should take into account the special capacities and advantages of the trial judge and pay appropriate deference where the opportunity for direct observation is likely to make a difference. Thus, on the accepted view that observed demeanor of a witness is a highly pertinent datum for appraising credibility, appellate courts will rarely substitute their own credibility determinations for those of the trial judge. For this and related reasons, the trial judge's findings of fact are not readily reversed, the formula familiar in the federal courts and many others being that such findings are upheld unless "clearly erroneous." This does not mean fact findings are unreviewable. It means only that upon review they are not easily or lightly reversible. Similarly, the trial judge's unique opportunity to observe the defendant may affect the style and scope of review, but need not and should not preclude review altogether.

The talk about sentencing lying in "discretion," and thus outside "law," bundles together a complex of conceptions and misconceptions that goes far to summarize the evils of the system. It is true that as we now handle this enormous power, trial judges are invited to proceed by hunch, by unspoken prejudice, by untested assumptions, and not by "law." But that is, as I have argued, the crux of what is wrong, not an argument for keeping things as they are. Correctly understood, the "discretion" of judicial officers in our system is not a blank check for arbitrary fiat. It is an authority, *within the law,* to weigh and appraise diverse factors (lawfully knowable factors) and make a responsible judgment, undoubtedly with a measure of latitude and finality varying according to the nature and scope of the discretion conferred. But "discretionary" does not mean "unappealable." Discretion may be abused, and discretionary decisions may be reversed for abuse.

The contention that sentencing is not regulated by rules of "law" subject to appellate review is an argument for, not against, a system of appeals. The "common law" is, after all, a body of rules evolved through the process of reasoned decision of concrete cases, mainly by appellate courts. English appellate courts and some of our states have been evolving general, legal "principles of sentencing" in the course of reviewing particular sentences claimed to be excessive.* One way to begin to temper the capricious unruliness of sentencing is to institute the right of appeal, so that appellate courts may proceed in their accustomed fashion to make law for this grave subject.

I describe this as "one way." It is not the only, or a sufficient, way. The world has changed greatly from the time of relative simplicity and slow movement when most law was the common law made by judges. Speed and complexity have required exponential increases in legislative action. Comparable needs call for extensive study and action by the Con-

* David A. Thomas, *Principles of Sentencing* (London, Heinemann Educational Books, Ltd., 1970) is a scholar's synthesis of the propositions gleaned from English decisions of "appeals against sentence" during the period from January 1962 to October 1969.

gress and the state legislatures to govern the field of sentencing. I shall add some broad-stroke thoughts about this later on. For now, however, recognizing that the events of politics and government do not march in single straight lines, I merely mention an awareness of the pervasive interrelatedness. The enactment of legislation makes appellate review simpler (with more precise guidelines) and narrows the area open for judicial lawmaking. The fashioning of reasonably specific rules may have the effect ultimately of making appellate review less urgently necessary—though we do not deny appeals where the law is relatively precise and detailed.

But abandoning all the permutations the future may bring, I stump here for appellate review of sentences as one step toward the rule of law in a quarter where lawless and unchecked power has reigned for too long.

8

Indeterminate Sentences

WE ARE ALL amused these days by the mechanistic simplemindedness of the idea that the punishment should "fit the crime." It is part of our self-confessed greater sophistication that judgments far more subtle and detailed must be made in the specific case of each unique criminal. The sophistication has been developing, and reflected, during the last hundred years or so in the widespread movement toward "indeterminate" sentences. The quoted word is not used uniformly. I shall use it here, rather loosely, to describe any prison sentence for which the precise term of confinement is not known on the day of judgment but will be subject within a substantial range to the later decision of a parole board or some comparable agency under whatever name.

There are, under varying federal and state laws, varying degrees of indeterminacy. Skipping details, the Adult Authority in California is empowered, after "sentencing" in court, to set a maximum term in many cases of anything from a year to life. This means, of course, that the judge in effect merely pronounces the category of crime, leaving the actual sentence almost entirely for the administrative authorities. In our federal system, as a general rule (subject, like all legal things, to qualifications and exceptions), the Board of Parole has discretion to order release of the defendant at any point between completion of one-third and two-thirds of the sentence imposed by the judge.* Other states have other varieties of this sort of pattern.

The basic premise of the indeterminate sentence is the relatively modern conception that individualized rehabilitation is the paramount goal in sentencing. The idea is to avoid the Procrustean mold of uniform sentences to fit crimes in the abstract and to focus upon the progress over time of the particular individual so as to determine when it may be safe for society, and good for him, to set him free, at least within the limits of parole supervision. At the same time, the power given to a single parole agency may be expected to mitigate the disparities in sentencing caused by the unregulated vagaries of individual judges. While it has not been advanced as a primary justification for the indeterminate sentence, this seeming power of equalization appears to be at least one among the conceptions of their functions entertained by parole boards.

The goals of flexibility and evenhandedness seem compellingly worthy. To the extent that these goals are pursued by giving power to parole boards, the result is a corresponding loss of effective authority by sentencing judges. And we all know the familiar habit of officials to cling to power. Despite that, judges have not lately been heard to oppose, but often extol, the indeterminate sentence. In part, this reflects a genuine distaste for the grim responsibility of sentencing.

* Generally, again with exceptions, a federal prisoner becomes eligible for parole after serving one-third of his sentence. If he earns the usual amount of credit for good behavior ("good time"), he is entitled to be released as a matter of right after serving approximately two-thirds of his sentence. Hence, the generalization that the parole board's discretion ranges during the middle third—say from the fourth through the sixth year of a nine-year sentence.

A related sentiment is a sometimes-conceded sense of inadequacy, generating a relieved willingness to defer to the supposed expertise of parole officials.

The judges are by no means alone in such favorable sentiments. The movement toward indeterminacy in sentencing is broad and powerful. Scholars of the first rank have joined and propelled it. A prestigious and influential scholarly product, the Model Penal Code, provides for broadly indeterminate sentences. A number of state legislatures, including several influenced by the Model Penal Code, have opted for indeterminacy in recent revisions of their laws.

Until the last couple of years, the trend toward indeterminate sentencing has seemed irresistible. Just recently, from the prisons and elsewhere, some voices of dissent have been heard. I have come to believe that this minority position is sound and that indeterminate sentencing, as thus far employed and justified, has produced more cruelty and injustice than the benefits its supporters envisage.

Before undertaking to particularize this position, let me state it with somewhat greater care. I do not condemn the indeterminate sentence always and everywhere. My strictures have nothing to do, either, with such devices as "good time" or "industrial time"—the reductions a prisoner may earn for behaving well or working while confined. My thoughts, briefly capsulized here and spelled out below, are that:

> Vagueness and uncertainty in the law are (as I have urged earlier) prima facie evils, which does not mean they may never be tolerated, but does mean they call always for justification.
>
> There is no sound justification for a general and uniform system of indeterminacy, and the use of this idea across-the-board has blocked or concealed the need for concrete justification in specific cases where indeterminate sentences may conceivably make sense.
>
> In our easy adoration of expertise, we have given over

power to people of dubious qualifications, subjected to little or no control.

We have subjected the supposed beneficiaries of the rehabilitative process to a hated regime of uncertainty and helplessness, ignoring that a program of "cures" thus imposed is doomed from its inception.

The case for the indeterminate sentence rests, initially, upon a laudable concern for each unique individual, coupled with a frequently baseless assumption that we are able effectively to understand and uniquely to "treat" the individual. The offender is "sick," runs the humane thought, and/or dangerous. He needs to be helped and "cured." Nobody, certainly not the sentencing judge, can know when he will be well and no more dangerous than the masses of us who are lucky enough not to have been convicted. Hence, those charged with "treatment" must be left to decide the time for release.

This "rehabilitative ideal," as a noted legal scholar has tagged and criticized it,* is genetically flawed and malformed. Its first dubiety is the fallacious—or, at least, far too broad—assumption that criminals are "sick" in some way that calls for "treatment." Of course, if you say blandly that nobody commits a serious crime unless he is "sick," the proposition is a useless tautology. To be meaningful in our context, the statement must be that (1) the person has some identifiable disorder apart from the mere biographical datum of his offense, (2) the disorder in some verifiable (or theoretically refutable) way ** is causally related to the offense,

* Francis A. Allen, *The Borderland of Criminal Justice* (Chicago, University of Chicago Press, 1964), pp. 25–41.

** To labor what most readers will find obvious, when I say a meaningful proposition must be "theoretically refutable," I intend the now familiar point that it must be possible to state for the proposition the conditions for establishing its falsity. Thus, the "law" that "all gases expand when heated" is meaningful in this sense because it would be refuted when and if we heated a gas that did not then expand.

and (3) the penologists or judges or somebody in authority knows some way and place for treatment of the disorder. Formulated in this testable way, the theory fails on at least a couple of weighty grounds.

We sentence many people every day who are not "sick" in any identifiable respect and are certainly not candidates for any form of therapy or "rehabilitation" known thus far. Many convicted criminals fall within a class labeled in one lively, psychoanalytically oriented book as "normal criminals." * This is a group who, as nearly as anyone can perceive, are not driven by, or "acting out," neurotic or psychotic impulses. Instead, they have coldly and deliberately figured the odds, risked punishment for rewards large enough (in their view) to justify the risk, but then had the misfortune to be caught. It seems likely that many of those in organized crime fall within this category. The same is true for large numbers (though by no means all) of those who scheme to defraud, to evade taxes, to counterfeit the currency, or to commit other varieties of acquisitive crime. (Definitely excluded, to illustrate the thick mysteries of the whole subject, are the check forgers, whose numbers appear to include a large proportion of disturbed people, driven by compulsions far deeper than greed.) The "normal criminal," whatever else he may need or merit, is not a promising candidate for any sort of treatment available in our prisons, our hospitals, or any other known institution.

Another facet of the case, abstractly separate but not easy to keep always separate in fact, is the severely limited character of our ability to treat the supposedly sick criminal. As to the theoretical separability of this point, there is no strain in distinguishing the idea of disease from that of cure. We know of identified diseases, some deadly, for which we know no cure. In the field of criminology, however, where ig-

* Franz Alexander and Hugo Staub, *The Criminal, the Judge and the Public* (Glencoe, Ill., The Free Press, 1956), pp. 81–2, 96, 107, 139–49, 209–11.

norance reigns so nearly absolute, the distinction is blurred. The apostles of rehabilitation and indeterminate sentences posit "sickness" without identifying its character and then urge "treatment" no better defined or specified. The absence of treatment or facilities—is by itself a fatal defect for purposes of the present discussion. However useful it may be elsewhere to identify incurable diseases, there is no justification for a regime of rehabilitation through indeterminate sentences unless we have some substantial hope or prospect of rehabilitating. Our subject is, after all, the confinement of people for long and uncertain periods of time. It is an evil to lock people up. There may be compensating goods that warrant it. But a mythical goal of rehabilitation is no good at all.

The myth, as I shall continue to urge here, is much more than an objectionable abstraction. It is the foundation, however well surrounded with good intentions, upon which we construct a monstrous apparatus of ignorance and horror. Consider the implications of a small, rather commonplace, undramatic illustration. Early in 1972, a highly regarded, earnest, professionally trained official was installed as New York City's Correction Commissioner. According to the front page of *The New York Times* for January 20, 1972, the new commissioner made a pledge of "enlightened treatment," saying:

> All men are redeemable. Every man can be rehabilitated, and it's up to us in the community and in the field of criminal justice to see that this is done.

With all deference to the commissioner, and acknowledging his apparent general qualifications, the quoted expressions are unsound and (all unintentionally) pernicious. Assuming it means something, the assertion that "all men are redeemable" promises to remain undemonstrated long after I and even the commissioner are gone. Assuming it means about the same thing, the same observation goes for the pronouncement that "every man can be rehabilitated." It is not disagreeable for people "in the community and in the field of criminal justice," assuming they have no more pressing things to do, to devote their energies to the attempted proof or accomplishment of universal redeemability. What is disagreeable—and vicious—is to cage prisoners for indeterminate stretches while we set about their assured rehabilitation, not knowing what to do for them or, really, whether we can do any useful thing for them.

Having imported the supposed model of sickness-and-cure with a simpleminded lack of discrimination, the proponents of indeterminate sentences actually misconceive the medical analogy. The physician, when he undertakes a cure or treatment procedure, is usually not indeterminate to any large extent in forecasting the time required. When you check in for an appendectomy or brain surgery, or for hepatitis or mononucleosis, it is generally possible to predict within reasonable limits how long before you will be out, one way or another. There are exceptions: psychotherapy, perhaps the most relevant analogy, tends to be among them. But even here, where there exists some approximately known approach to "rehabilitation," the idea of broad indeterminacy is not in general medical vogue. With indeterminate prison sentences, however, the approach to time predictions is neither sought nor attainable. Having in view no genuine program of "treatment," the sentencers and parole officers cannot say how long it will take. What happens in practical fact is that we think in imposing an indeterminate sentence we are following the Correction Commissioner's precept to see to the defendant's redemption; we send the prisoner away for as long as that consummation may require, not knowing when or whether it may be achieved; and we go on to the next case borne on a vaporous sense of virtue and justice.

In this state of blissfully ignorant cruelty, we dump into our generally huge prisons unsorted varieties of prisoners—

the few who may need treatment we know how to supply, the many we don't know how to treat, whatever they may need, and the many more who evidence no perceptible need for treatment, existing or imagined. This is the macabre but not astonishing culmination of an indeterminate-sentencing process that rests mainly upon fiction and absentmindedness. The sentence purportedly tailored to the cherished needs of the individual turns out to be a crude order for simple warehousing. The prison characteristically has no treatment facilities of any substantial nature. The means for rehabilitation, undefined and probably unknown, are not at hand. How could they be if they have not been identified, let alone supplied?

Thus, while we pour increasing numbers of people into prisons for the serving of uncertain sentences, the most basic of asserted justifications, the program of rehabilitation, is absent. In a host of cases, then, when somebody says a prisoner must stay locked up because he is not "ready" for release, the ultimate Kafkaism is the lack of any definition of "ready." Facing the facts, we know that "treatment" is mostly an illusion in our prisons. There is powerful evidence that the majority of prisoners deteriorate—become poorer risks and lesser people—rather than improve in prison. This is certainly the case for sentences dragging on beyond four or five years, which includes a huge number, especially among highly indeterminate sentences. It is bracing doctrine, of course, whether or not it makes sense, to insist, as many do, that our prisons must be improved to make rehabilitation a reality. Assuming that is feasible—assuming we can on any scale rehabilitate people while keeping them locked up—the point of transcending consequence at the moment is that we are not doing so. Because we are not, the main prop for indeterminate sentences is a hollow reed. Unless we mean to make sadist jokes, we cannot fairly send people away for "as long as it takes" to be rehabilitated, then merely hold them until a whimsical release date, doing nothing meanwhile that pretends to be rehabilitative.

The quality of horrid joke manifests itself in more than one way. It appears every time we impose an indeterminate sentence on a defendant who is patently not a subject for any kind of rehabilitation. Examples will come to mind quickly. Think of the prominent businessman convicted of tax evasion, the high political official guilty of taking bribes, the union leader condemned for embezzlement. Assume, if concrete cases do not recall themselves to you right away, that these are men of advanced years. People like this are not rationally to be deemed candidates for "treatment"; their sentences are for punishment—whether viewed as a way of deterring them, deterring others, or even for retribution. There is no place in the indeterminate-sentencing theory for cases of this kind. There are no relevant questions a parole board could ask in deciding when to end a term of imprisonment for such defendants. Yet, with increasing frequency, as more penal codes embrace the unqualified rule of indeterminate sentences, defendants like them are being sent away for uncertain terms, to await the unpredictable, unexplained, and unexplainable pleasure of the parole board.

The reference in this connection to parole boards spotlights another gruesome aspect of the indeterminacy regime. It is widely believed, in prison and out, that parole boards operate without orderly and uniform criteria for judgment, often moved by "political" pressures or the winds of public opinion, without the benefit of mature and organized wisdom. There are grounds for such beliefs, based upon what parole officials and scholars have told us, and perhaps even more upon the heavy blanket of silence and mystery under which these agencies carry on. The United States Board of Parole is probably among the best organizations of its kind. Yet a noted legal scholar, not given to hyperbole, concluded after wide study: "The performance of the Parole Board seems on the whole about as low in quality as anything I have seen in the federal government." *

Nobody has tried lately in our community to dispute Lord Acton's perception concerning the corrupting influence of absolute power. Knowing the danger, we have not worried about it in handing over prisoners to the unguided discretion of parole officials. We have allowed and encouraged those officials to think like tyrants—possibly benevolent, but tyrants none the less. Writing as late as March 1972, the then Chairman of the United States Board of Parole found it appropriate to declaim in a professional journal that under federal law "parole is a matter of 'grace' and not of 'right.' " ** The statement was not sound or intelligible law when it was made. But the author had been accustomed to think of himself as a dispenser of grace, not a respecter of rights, and that has epitomized the reality of parole-board functioning for a long time.

It would be unfair and inaccurate to conclude that the major ill in this quarter is the inferiority or bad disposition of parole officials. Taken all together, they are—like judges and others—merely human. Because their roles are vaguely defined, their qualifications are inevitably uncertain. Many of them, assigned without guidance to answer unintelligible questions, work hard and earnestly for small rewards. But the system is unworkable. Given the foggy terms of their mandate, parole boards give us no less than we have a right to expect. We charge them to make indeterminate sentences determinate, but we give them no conceptual or other tools to work with. We set them lofty goals of rehabilitation, but with no directions or means of achievement. We set the scene,

* Kenneth Culp Davis, *Discretionary Justice* (Baton Rouge, Louisiana State University Press, 1969), p. 133.

** George J. Reed and William E. Amos, "Improved Parole Decision-Making," *Federal Probation* (March 1972), p. 16. Chairman Reed stepped aside a few months later, remaining, however, as a board member while turning over the chair to a colleague.

in short, so that an honest official would often be incapable of explaining on rational, principled grounds why on a certain day Union Official A and Bribed Legislative Aide B were granted parole, while the applications of Perjurious Politician C and Swindler D were denied. Then we flagellate the officials for announcing the decisions as unexplained ukases.

And what of the alleged beneficiaries of the rehabilitative ideal, the prisoners? How do they respond to the boon of indeterminate sentences? A former Attorney General of the United States has extolled the indeterminate sentence as an attractive incentive, contrasting favorably with the gray inexorability of a fixed term.* A United States Attorney, who has since become a Federal District Judge, put the same point this way:

> Inherent in the indeterminate sentence procedure is the stimulation of an offender's incentive towards rehabilitation. He is aware that under the program designed for him there will be periodic revaluations of his potential for parole, and that he will return to the community only when his attitudes and patterns of behavior have been sufficiently modified." **

However good "stimulation" and "incentive" may sound to prosecutors and others on the outside, it does not detonate echoes inside prison walls. The growing evidences of prisoner sentiment—which introspection and conversation lead me to find persuasive—indicate that the inmate experiences as cruel and degrading the command that he remain in custody for some uncertain period, while his keepers study him, grade him in secret, and decide if and when he may be let go. I think this should not surprise us. Harking back to a point made early in this book, it is pertinent again to recall how deeply we prize certainty and predictability in the workings of the law. We want to be able to plan our businesses and

* Ramsey Clark, *Crime in America* (New York, Pocket Books, 1971), p. 203.

** Matthew Byrne, Jr., "Federal Sentencing Procedures: Need for Reform," 42 *Los Angeles Bar Bulletin,* pp. 563, 567 (1967).

family decisions by knowing in advance just how painful the tax will be, what the zoning laws promise, how long an employment contract will endure. It may be imagined that knowing the actual length of a prison term might serve similar, though much more searing, needs.

At any rate, prisoners and students of their plight so testify. The uncertainty of the indeterminate sentence is experienced as a steadily galling affliction. There is a sense of helpless rage which is enhanced by a prevalent disbelief in the reality of rehabilitation as a goal. "How," writes one rehabilitee in California, "do you rehabilitate a cat who has never been 'habilitated'?" * Brooding and skeptical, wondering when he will be released, the same prisoner writes: "He can only guess. And this guessing game only infuriates him and increases his distrust of the penal system." ** As to the absolute control of California's Adult Authority over the actual time to be served, he says: "No such power should be in the hands of a few men." † To cite only one more example of what appears to be a prevalent feeling, a set of inmate grievances during a November 1971 riot in a New Jersey prison included this near the top: "Rahway Prison is a place where you never know how to make parole." ‡

For those wondering when the miracle may happen, there is a desperate sense of mystery about what the rules are, most centrally about what will "work" toward the tensely focused goal of release. There is a bitter, and seemingly growing, conviction that a craven conformity is the key. The silence surrounding parole-board decisions nurtures cynicism among the prisoners—a belief in the arbitrariness and essential corruption of those in power. A pervasive sense of helplessness generates frustration and rage.

* Prisoner Alfred Hassan in Eve Pell, ed., *Maximum Security—Letters from California's Prisons* (New York, Dutton and Co., 1972), p. 22.

** *Ibid.*, p. 31.

† *Ibid.*, p. 33.

‡ *The New York Times* (November 27, 1971), p. 18.

These sentiments are important data in themselves. Even if we knew much about how to rehabilitate, the hostility of those invited grandly to be "redeemed" would be a countervailing force of some magnitude. The trouble is compounded if, as I believe, the hostility responds to a system that is misconceived, harsh, and oppressive in its operation.

Trained in legal forensics, I have assailed somewhat robustly the prevalent theses of rehabilitation and indeterminate sentences. I do not deem it appropriate to mute these attacks. But their dimensions should not be obscured in the rhetoric. It is not my claim that rehabilitation is always and everywhere impossible. Nor do I argue that an indeterminate sentence could never be wise and fair. The great evil in current thinking is the pair of false assumptions that (1) rehabilitation is *always* possible and (2) indeterminate sentences are *always* desirable. I urge that the shoe belongs on the other foot. Most importantly, my contention is that the presumption ought always to be in favor of a definite sentence, known and justified on the day of sentencing (and probably much shorter than our sentences tend to run). There should be a burden of justifying an indeterminate sentence in any particular case—a burden to be satisfied only by concrete reasons and a concrete program for the defendant in that case. The justifications, I tentatively suggest (subject to the organized thought and study urged in the next chapter), would consist of identified needs and resources for effective rehabilitation or for incapacitation of a dangerous offender, or both.

To be slightly more concrete, there are specific kinds of defendants for whom we have plausible, if by no means certain, hopes of rehabilitation. It appears, for example, that there are some meaningful hypotheses about "treatment" for some drug users, some sex offenders, and, most hopefully, some of our numerous young offenders. Even as to these, the hopes must be modest, scaled to the meagerness of our knowledge and our niggardliness in allocating resources to such concerns. Other kinds of specific cases could be added. Most judges and penologists can recall rare but exceedingly rewarding instances in which genuine help has seemingly saved an offender from further misery to himself and the community. Cases of this sort include some in which the delicate, difficult judgment has been made to remove a young delinquent from an emotionally diseased home and where the miracle of effective parenting elsewhere has been achievable. One case in my recollection, scarcely unique but altogether gratifying, involved a young man whose string of offenses has been ended (at least, strictly speaking, broken for some years) after repair of a harelip notably improved his appearance, his speech, and, above all, his estimate of himself. Others with much greater knowledge could supply a large catalogue of comparable examples—cases where concrete diagnoses and real treatment appear to have been feasible and effective.

Moreover, having railed against the airy nonsense that everyone can be rehabilitated, I would not insist that certainty of success be a precondition for the attempt. In the field of drug abuse, to illustrate in terms of what may be our most harrowing problem today, there are competing ideas about treatment, with no clear case of efficacy made for any of them. So here, as in several kinds of more purely "medical" effort, programs of treatment go forward in what ought to be seen candidly as courses of trial-and-error testing. But the uncertainty is not grounds for abandoning the effort. Unlike grand inanities about universal redemption, narcotics programs center upon a reasonably well-identified and defined species of pathology. The several modes of treatment are describable in terms that have meaning and tolerable limits, including, importantly, limits upon the time required for achieving success or admitting failure. It is significant, too, that the subject admits of intelligible discourse about "success" and "failure"; it is possible to identify results or their absence with a decent approach to precision. Finally, programs for treatment of addicts are characteristically, though not always, built upon the patient's acquiescence. The willing participant seeking a shared objective is a pole away from the subject of an indeterminate sentence ostensibly justified by rehabilitative objectives for which he has been shown neither the need nor the means of achievement.

I have mentioned, but thus far only briefly, the additional thought that indeterminate sentences may be appropriate for the so-called "dangerous offender." This is far from a wholly separate topic from that of rehabilitation. The addict-mugger, the wantonly violent robber, the youth for whom an automobile, stolen if necessary, is somehow involved with machismo, the assaultive sex offender—individuals in such categories may be candidates for treatment because they are dangerous and because their disorders generate the danger. There is a wide and respectable, but risky and troublesome, trend to enact statutes for dangerous offenders authorizing long but indeterminate sentences. The risks and the disquietude are familiar in the relevant professions, though the appraisals are, as always, widely disparate. Most of those with knowledge are skeptical about the possibility of identifying with reasonable accuracy the dangerous individual. It is easy to err on the side of overcaution, resolving doubts in favor of confinement. But while that appears in fact to have happened on a large scale, nobody worth listening to commends it as a happy course for a civilized society.

If we know—or knew—how to detect who is dangerous, the theory of indeterminate sentences proceeds into the succeeding question, equally shrouded in ignorance: how do we judge when the danger has been sufficiently alleviated so that the defendant should be released? We can, of course (and often do), hold the violent offender until he is old and feeble, but this is only an extension of the unacceptable excess mentioned above. What we would want, and mostly lack, are some reliable tests for predicting behavior in relevant respects. A main criterion, the assessment of behavior in prison, seems almost by definition to be unreliable. The prisoner who conforms and seems "adjusted" in close confinement with minimal autonomy may be exhibiting qualities that expose him as unfit for effective functioning on the outside.

Granting the difficulties, including the recurrent agonies of weighing imponderable risks and the demands for security against our professed preference for liberty, there is probably a suitable ground for indeterminate sentencing in the service of incapacitating dangerous people. Where the questions are close, I would think our constitutional commitments to freedom would entail the acceptance of more risk than a different society might deem bearable. However specific cases might go, the need for incapacitation and the criteria for continuing scrutiny should be specified with maximum feasible particularity. And I know as I write such words—"maximum feasible particularity"—what a vague and dubious message they convey. But I am here making a reluctant concession, not urging a program. It may be that the concession, after the desperately needed study of such matters, will be proved foolish. If so, I would be pleased to retract it.

Subject, then, to more wisdom later, let me reiterate my basic thoughts about indeterminate sentences: they are usually evil and unwarranted, but they may be suitable upon detailed showings in specific cases involving (1) demonstrated needs for rehabilitation and incapacitation and (2) rationally organized means for serving those needs. Otherwise, and for the great majority of cases, sentences ought to be stated with maximum certainty, based almost entirely upon factors known on the day of sentencing, and determined with the nearest approach we can make to objective, equal, and "impersonal" evaluation of the relevant qualities of both the criminal and the crime. The large dimensions of these last observations are meant only to suggest a large agenda for years to come. A few more particulars of that proposed work are the main business of the next chapter, the final one of this book.

9

Proposals for the Lawmakers

THE ARBITRARY cruelties perpetrated daily under our existing sentencing practices are not easy to reconcile with the cardinal principles of our Constitution. The largely unbridled powers of judges and prison officials stir questions under the clauses promising that life and liberty will not be denied except by "due process of law." The crazy quilt of disparities—the wide differences in treatment of defendants whose situations and crimes look similar and whose divergent sentences are unaccounted for—stirs doubts as to whether the guarantee of the "equal protection of the laws" is being fulfilled.

While I mean mostly to avoid constitutional questions that may lie just over the legal horizon, it is scarcely possible to omit some reference to the Supreme Court decision of June 29, 1972, outlawing capital punishment in at least the existing modes of administering that ultimate penalty.* Four of the five Justices comprising the bare majority (in the separate opinion each wrote) attached substantial or dispositive weight to the fact that the death penalty has been "arbitrarily," "dis-

* *Furman* v. *Georgia,* 408 U.S. 238.

criminatorily," "capriciously" imposed. "Wanton" and "freakish" were among the words Mr. Justice Stewart used. The choice between who lives and who must die, observed Mr. Justice Brennan, "smacks of little more than a lottery system." Whether the decision on the death sentence was for the judge or (in many states) for the jury, the absence of criteria or explanations left, in Mr. Justice White's view, "no meaningful basis for distinguishing the few cases in which it is imposed from the many cases in which it is not." Similarly, stressing the open door to discrimination against the poor or against racial minorities, Mr. Justice Douglas denounced the reign of "untrammeled discretion" subject to no known or stated "standards." As many commentators have observed, these qualities of accident and caprice were in the last analysis the vital grounds of decision, so that, at least in theory, a rational and equally applied law imposing the death penalty could still find a Supreme Court majority to sustain it.

I repeat my intention to resist speculations in the field of constitutional law. Reluctantly turning from the capital-punishment decision, I merely register the view that the central point about whimsical and unequal sentencing is in principle germane in non-capital cases. This could mean one day that the Supreme Court might deem itself constrained finally to move more broadly, on constitutional grounds, against the kinds of "wanton and freakish" disparities I (and so many others) have deplored. What it ought also to mean—preferably and more directly and immediately—is that those with the primary responsibility for governing in a democratic society have now been supplied with an enlightening reminder of concerns too long neglected. I refer, of course, to our elected lawmakers, who are, not less than the judges, bound by their oaths to support the Constitution. But the oath is scarcely the heart of the matter. It remains the essence and the hope of our polity that those we elect should be taking the lead in our efforts to civilize ourselves through law. The creative potential of the judges in a complex society is narrow and interstitial for most purposes. They can—and I refer, naturally, to our Supreme Court as the essential organ in this respect—state and seek to improve the broad principles. But the continuous shaping and staffing of the working institutions must depend upon the apparatus of executive and legislative leadership.

Believing, then, that there is need for broad and drastic reform of the law, I devote this final chapter to some legislative proposals. The ideas set out here are tentative, as must be any one person's ideas offered as grist for the long, slow, deliberate mills of legislative action. They are also incomplete, as must be any proposals in a slender volume touching a subject so huge, involved, and troubled as that of criminal sanctions. While the discussion below begins with some specifics, the main goal of this effort is not to argue for definitive solutions, but to suggest lines of inquiry, debate, and experimentation. Let us begin.

SOME SPECIFICS

The Lawful Purposes of Sanctions

A Supreme Court opinion in 1958 made the obvious point that the "apportionment of punishment," its "severity," "its efficacy or its futility," all "are peculiarly questions of legislative policy." * Fully agreeing that this *ought to be* so, I have been saying at some length that the legislature has for too long abdicated this basic function. To begin at the elementary beginning, we have an almost entire absence in the United States of legislative determinations—of "law"—governing the basic questions as to the purposes and justifications of criminal sanctions. Without binding guides on such questions, it is inevitable that individual sentencers will

* *Gore* v. *United States,* 357 U.S. 386, 393.

strike out on a multiplicity of courses chosen by each decision-maker for himself. The result is chaos.

The writings of philosophers and lawyers about sentencing have identified a familiar small list of purposes to be sought through the imposition of criminal sanctions. There is not universal agreement on the list. There are bookshelves of disputation concerning the feasibility or moral propriety of one asserted objective or another. Skirting that interesting subject, let me just note for present uses the main ends of criminal sentences that have been posited at one time or another:

Retribution, the exaction of payment—"an eye for an eye."

Deterrence, which may be "general" (i.e., discouraging others than the defendant from committing the wrong), "special" (discouraging the specific defendant from doing it again), or both.

Denunciation, or condemnation—as a symbol of distinctively criminal "guilt," as an affirmation and re-enforcement of moral standards, and as reassurance to the law-abiding.

Incapacitation, during the time of confinement.

Rehabilitation or *reformation* of the offender.

Different scholars would shorten or lengthen the list, or prefer other terminology. While the academic debate continues, it is ignored by those empowered (and expected) to make uniform rules of law. We have in our country virtually no legislative declarations of the principles justifying criminal sanctions. It will take only a minute or two to show that this is much more than an aesthetically regrettable lack. It is the omission of foundation stones, without which no stable or reliable structure is possible.

To begin at the first item on the debatable list, there is in contemporary jurisprudential literature a large majority for, but a vocal minority against, the view that retribution is not an acceptable aim of sentencing. There are judges, naturally, on both sides of the issue. While that is to be expected, the power of the judges to go their variable and conflicting ways in sentencing is not tolerable. And it is perfectly clear that divergent opinions on the purposes of punishment will lead to divergent decisions as to the appropriate sentence. We expect judges, like others, to hold varying opinions on many things—on the scope and limits of permissible wiretapping, on the desirability of outlawing gambling, on bank loans for securities purchases, on prostitution, whatever. But we neither expect nor permit that each judge should follow his private judgment in deciding the legal consequences of these—or any—forms of conduct. The consequences are matters of law, prescribed legislatively and equally for all.

It seems clear to me that judgments affecting consequences so grave as the length and character of sentences should similarly be matters of law. Whatever our individual preferences may be, it is for the legislature in our system to decide and prescribe the legitimate bases for criminal sanctions. Accordingly, while it may remain a matter for debate and amendment in the future, there ought to be one uniform rule now on such questions as whether retribution is a legitimate concept to be entertained by a judge in determining a sentence. There should be at a minimum a basic provision of the criminal code listing and defining the legislatively decreed purposes or objectives the community has chosen to pursue, for the time being, by means of criminal sanctions.

The utility of such elementary provisions seems plain to me without indulging any illusions about absolute efficacy. Judges whose clearheadedness and integrity may not always be perfect will surely stray on occasion and allow themselves to be influenced by considerations excluded or forbidden by the code. We may be sure this happens now, to some uncertain extent, with respect to all sorts of statutory mandates. Nevertheless, we have wagered our destiny in considerable measure on the faith that officials, judicial and other, will do their duty far more often than not. My own observation and belief, perhaps not exquisitely objective, is that judges are powerfully moved most of the time, by habit and the moral pressures of their profession, to hew to the law as they are able to perceive it. I think, to be quite specific, most judges would be committed all the time to quell private preferences and enforce fully a set of legislative standards declaring what ends are—and what ends are not—allowably sought in criminal sentences.

Building upon this premise, I would go on to project that an important train of consequences would follow directly from legislative definitions of sentencing objectives. Along with the declaration of sentencing purposes, the legislature would—certainly it should—provide that the judge (or sentencing tribunal) must state which among the allowable purposes were the supposed bases for each particular sentence. The simple requirement would compel the judge to think connectedly about his reasons and to justify explicitly decisions now taken on unarticulated hunches. It would facilitate, as I will show in a minute, the beginnings of rational choices between definite and indeterminate sentences. And it would open the way for intelligent scrutiny on appeal since an appellate court can function usefully only when it knows the grounds of the decision brought to it for review.

To illustrate these points, let us hypothesize a sentencing code with an initial section declaring the permissible objects of sentencing. Suppose the list is the one I tendered awhile ago: retribution, deterrence ("general" and "special"), denunciation, incapacitation, and rehabilitation. Assume that the sentencer must decide and state which of these purposes underlie the judgment in each individual case. Assume, finally, that the system is to include both definite and indeterminate sentences—i.e., some to be fixed in length at the time of sentencing, others to be fixed finally by later decisions of a parole board.

One clear benefit of such provisions would be a long step toward sense and rationality in choosing for the particular case between the two kinds of sentences. If the sentencer determines that the particular case implicates the goals of general deterrence and, perhaps, retribution—and determines at the same time that the defendant is neither dangerous nor a suitable candidate for rehabilitation—there should be no occasion for an indeterminate sentence. Whatever complexities and imponderables there are—and there are plenty, some to be touched upon below—there is none that is not knowable on the day of sentencing. Or, to note the other side of the coin, there is none that is justifiably postponed for, or assigned to, parole-board consideration. There are no factors or questions peculiarly suited—or, indeed, suited at all—to handling by the supposed expertise of parole officials. The impact of the sentence in such a case is presumably achieved in the very fact, and at the very time, of its pronouncement. Assuming, of course, that sentences are known to be carried out, the effect of the example on other people is achieved and the desire for vengeance is satisfied without regard to the kinds of treatment and observation to which the prisoner is thereafter subjected. It is arguable, in fact, that indeterminacy in such a case is unsound, quite apart from its oppressive impact upon the defendant. Since the effects for general deterrence and retribution are really aimed at people other than the defendant himself, uncertainty in the sentence tends to diminish or dissipate its impact.

To elaborate this simple analysis a little more, take the case where the sentencer has studied the defendant and found concrete needs for incapacitation and rehabilitation. This, of course, presents the arguable occasion for an indeterminate sentence. In this sort of case, the intended effect is upon the defendant and is to be achieved, in considerable measure at least, over some period of time, not at the instant of sentencing. The questions presented at the time of the sentence entail predictions: when, if ever, will the defendant's dangerous propensities subside? How soon may we hope to cure or alleviate the defects disposing him to violate the criminal law? Being in their nature risky predictions, the answers to such questions must be tentative, subject to later verification or correction.

It should be obvious that the purpose or purposes of a sentence are first steps toward deciding whether a definite or indeterminate term is appropriate. However obvious, the point is systematically ignored both in existing statutes prescribing penalties and in the current judgments of the courts. Existing codes, buttressed by still prevalent professional opinion, rarely make distinctions along the lines of purpose. They tend simply to provide for indeterminacy across the board. They do not call upon the sentencer even to consider, let alone to state, whether any rehabilitative or incapacitating goal is involved. There is no suggestion of what a parole board is to be looking at or looking for as it hears the prisoner's application for release. Small wonder that our parole boards characteristically never tell the prisoner—or anyone—the grounds of their decisions. Who knows if they know?

Without pretending to follow the whole course of implications and issues, we can readily see further stages of judgment after the choice between a definite and an indefinite sentence has been made. Where we seek only general deterrence, say, of tax evaders or bribetakers, we may come to see that relatively short but substantially inexorable sentences to prison are the prescription. More complex questions present themselves when we think the case involves a need or a desire for rehabilitation. It does not follow as a matter of good sense—though it appears currently to be a matter of practice—that such a sentence must or should be indeterminate. First off, it is not definitive that a judge (perhaps echoing, without deep insight, the debatable views of others) is led to say there is a need for rehabilitation. He may be wrong. If he is right, there is still the question whether and where appropriate rehabilitative resources may be found. It is a familiar kind of well-intended mockery for our judges to imagine vaguely, or to say, that psychotherapy or some other form of treatment is the proper course for a defendant, to impose a supposedly rehabilitative sentence, and to ignore that there is no pertinent treatment available where the defendant is sent or anywhere else in the state's penal facilities.

Compelled to focus on what he thinks he means by rehabilitation, the sentencer should be better able to know whether he really means it at all. He should be able to see with some clarity whether and why the sentence should be indeterminate. He should be moved to ask insistently where the defendant will be taken from the courtroom, what will be done to or for him, and why that course is thought to present realistic prospects of rehabilitation.

What I have done under the present heading is barely to sketch the kinds of effective assistance toward rational *classification* of sentences we might derive from formulating agreed purposes. The elaboration of this subject alone should be a task of large proportions for the future. Meaning here only to provoke initial thoughts—and, later on, to propose the organization of extensive research, study, and law reform—I leave the topic at this barely introduced stage.

Toward Codified Weights and Measures

However we prettify them by aspirations to redeem and regenerate, and whatever may come to pass someday, criminal penalties are painful measures taken against offenders for *punishment*. Indeed, moral philosophers of stature have insisted that in the last analysis, no other justification for criminal sanctions exists. We need not vote on that position to know what everyone knows—that we fine and jail and denounce people to punish them.

Recalling that elementary truism, we confront directly every man's first and main question about the sentence: how long or severe will it—should it—be? Our practice in this country, of which I have complained at length, is to leave that ultimate question to the wide, largely unguided, unstandardized, usually unreviewable judgment of a single official, the trial judge. This means, naturally, that intermediate questions as to factors tending to mitigate or to aggravate are also for that individual's exclusive judgment. We allow him not merely to "weigh" the various elements that go into a sentence. Prior to that, we leave to his unfettered (and usually unspoken) preferences the determination as to what factors ought to be considered at all, and in what direction. To a large extent, we have tended to justify this state of affairs on the unexamined belief that it is unavoidable because each individual case is a unique complexity of peculiar and "imponderable" attributes and circumstances. The position should, I think, be examined and changed.

As I have urged already, there is no valid reason for leaving to the individual judges their varying rules on what factors ought to be *material* and to what effect. To say something is "material" means it is legally significant. We know what is legally significant by consulting *the law*. We do not allow each judge to make up the law for himself on other questions. We should not allow it with respect to sentencing.

Let me particularize this again with examples already mentioned. It is a proposition of law to say that pleading guilty, rather than insisting upon the right to stand trial, will (or will not) be deemed a mitigating factor. It is another such proposition to say that the trial judge should (or should not) consider prior convictions as aggravating factors in sentencing. The same goes for the judge's perception of whether the defendant lied on the stand, engaged in disruptive behavior, or otherwise misbehaved at his trial. The list could be extended.

My point of departure, now familiar, is that judges entertain contradictory views on all such factors. My next point is one that should long ago have been established as self-evident: such things should be handled uniformly under legislative enactments.

Beyond codifying the numerous factors affecting the length or severity of sentences, an acceptable code of penal *law* should, in my judgment, prescribe guidelines for the application and assessment of these factors. While it may seem dry, technical, unromantic, and "mechanical," I have in mind the creation eventually of a detailed chart or calculus to be used (1) by the sentencing judge in weighing the many elements that go into the sentence; (2) by lawyers, probation officers, and others undertaking to persuade or enlighten the judge; and (3) by appellate courts in reviewing what the judge has done. Once more, I mean only to paint in broad strokes, leaving the matter for debate and, I would hope, development later on.

The sentencing judge commonly faces a decision within a huge range—for example, anything from probation to twenty-five years in prison for armed robbery of a federally insured bank. In deciding where to fix any particular sentence, he will presumably consider a host of factors in the case: the relative seriousness of the particular offense—the degree of danger threatened, cruelty, premeditation; the prior record of the defendant; situational factors—health, family disturbance, drug use; the defendant's work history, skills, potential; etc. In the existing mode of handling the sentence, the judge is under no pressure—and is without guidelines—toward systematic, exhaustive, detailed appraisal of such things one by one. He probably does not list them even for himself. He certainly does not record or announce the analysis. Probably, in most cases, he broods in a diffuse way toward a hunch that becomes a sentence. It may be a lenient or a harsh sentence. But even that cannot be stated with vivid meaning. Only other hunches, equally unstructured, supply the standards of comparison. And there is, of course, no explicit course of reasoning anyone—an appellate tribunal, for instance—could rationally approve or disapprove.

The partial remedy I propose is a kind of detailed profile or checklist of factors that would include, wherever possible, some form of numerical or other objective grading. Still being crude and cursory, I suggest that "gravity of offense" could be graded along a scale from, perhaps, 1 to 5. Other factors could be handled in the same way. The overall result might be a score—or, possibly, an individual profile of sentencing elements—that would make it feasible to follow the sentencer's estimates, criticize them, and compare the sentence in the given case with others.

The justification for such a technique does not require that we accept delusions of precision. Admittedly, "gravity of offense" does not lend itself to weighing with the mechanical simplicity of grocery or jewelers' scales. But we know from sufficiently analogous fields that numerical statements may serve, for obviously non-quantifiable subjects, as useful implements for clarification of thought, comparisons, and criticism. We know, for example, of wide uses in social research of numerical scales for expressing preferences and other attitudes. The physician who speaks of a grade-three heart murmur may not be reporting a measurement as precise as the number of feet in a yard. But he says a meaningful thing that informs and guides others professionally trained.

It must be noted that efforts to codify sentencing factors have been made without notable success in the past. For the most part, they have been the work of some devoted European scholars. Their failures, however, should stand not as demonstrations of impossibility but as helpful explorations to assist further strivings toward just and equal sentences. It is not necessary, or desirable, to imagine that sentencing can be completely computerized. At the same time, the possibility of using computers as an aid toward orderly thought in sentencing need not be discounted in advance. James V. Bennett, for years the able Director of the Federal Bureau of Prisons, noted the possibility some time ago. As that humane and sensitive student would still be the first to insist, this does not envisage the displacement of people by machines. The need for delicate and difficult judgments will remain for as long a future as is now imaginable. What will change, we might hope, is the uncharted expanse in which such judgments are now undertaken. We may hope to obtain some substantial degree of concrete agreement on concrete factors capable of being stated, discussed, and thought about in the style of a legal system for rational people rather than a lottery.

Legislative Judgments on Sentencing Procedures

I have dealt critically in earlier pages with various aspects of sentencing procedure—among others, the absence of review and the failure to adopt multimember tribunals. Matters like these are ripe subjects for legislative consideration. Recalling them in the present context, I will deal only with illustrative possibilities in the federal system.

Within that single national system, there is no reason for allowing variations to depend as much as they do upon the preferences of individual judges or courts. Appellate review of sentences, in addition to benefits even more important, would foster a measure of consistency and uniformity. Bills which would provide for such review, repeatedly introduced in recent years, should succeed. The favorable report of the American Bar Association (see Chapter 7) may tip the scale soon. If concerned citizens would enter the lists, success would be more certain, or at least swifter.

Other proposals for approaching uniformity and consistency through legislative action are entailed in views I have set forth. It is quaint, but not right, that the federal judges in metropolitan centers should decide for themselves, in differing ways, whether to employ such a technique as the sentencing council. Nobody has suggested anything unique in pertinent respects about the three federal courts—Detroit, Brooklyn, and Chicago—where sentencing councils operate. If the device is valuable in those places, it would be no less valuable in Manhattan (a ten-minute drive from Brooklyn), Boston, or Cleveland. If sentencing councils are undesirable—from the viewpoint, of course, of doing justice, not as a matter of judicial convenience—they ought not to exist anywhere. One way or another, this seems a subject clearly within legislative competence. There ought to be a national decision for the nation's courts on a matter of this kind.

When and if the need for uniform legislation is recognized, mixed tribunals of Professor Glueck's variety (one judge and two representatives of other professions) would be a possibility for study and debate. I have recorded my own preferences before now. What is far more important is that the time of ignoring such concerns should end and that there be the type of decision in Congress for which the Founders created power and responsibility in Articles I and III of our Constitution.*

Like all those whose business it is to work in the law, I could extend greatly my list of legislative suggestions. As has appeared, the apparatus of parole and parole-board procedures needs drastic revision. Around the time of this writing (in 1972) a subcommittee of the House Judiciary Committee has been conducting extensive hearings on this, as well as corrections practices in general, and we may hope for

* Article III creates the Supreme Court, but beyond that says only that there will be "such inferior courts as the Congress may from time to time ordain and establish." Article I authorizes Congress "To constitute Tribunals inferior to the supreme Court." Congress has broad powers, probably not unlimited, over both the jurisdiction and the procedure of the federal courts.

movement within a discernible future. The sentencing proceeding itself; the odd division of authority whereby judges sentence people for "treatment" over which the Attorney General, not the judges, has control; the conception and building of institutions other than the great gray prisons of the last two centuries—such large and small enterprises, among many others, should be on the legislative agenda.

The whole "system"—or, really, collection of disconnected pieces—of sentencing and corrections needs a program of coherent study and synthesis. The judges, for lack of time or talent or incentive, have not performed this task. The Congress could, or could direct its performance by the commission I shall propose shortly. Let me, very briefly, elaborate one of many possible illustrations of the need for connections and lines of communication. Under the federal law, since 1950 we have had special provisions for special treatment of youthful offenders. The idea, stated briefly, is to have facilities tailored to the qualities of the young people we hope to salvage—places for special training, counseling, guidance, etc. Sentences under these provisions are broadly indeterminate, and there is a goal proffered to the defendant of having his conviction erased from his record if his response is favorable. Trial judges are empowered to decide which defendants among those technically eligible should be sentenced as "youth offenders." While the statute book gives this authority to the judge, and while sentences under it are part of the district courts' daily output, the judge does not know, in fact, what will become of the defendant so sentenced. It is for the Attorney General, who is the chief prosecutor, and, more specifically, his Bureau of Prisons, to determine where the youth will be sent and for what. Though labeled a "youth offender" by the judge, any given defendant may find himself classified for standard adult treatment and sent to one of the regular prisons. In the given case, this may be absolutely sound; the judgment of the prison experts may be wiser than that of the judge. But the incongruous nullification of the sentence is cruel as well as silly. The judge, if he is to impose a sentence, ought to know the practical meaning and effect of what he pronounces. If the prison bureau is to be the actual sentencer, that ought to be clear and understood. If both are to collaborate, that should be known. What cannot be justified is the existence of an unconsidered veto power in those who are not commissioned, and not formally recognized, to exercise the sentencing power.

I have tarried over a single, and incomplete, need for the seeking of some sensible order in sentencing through law. A long and far more detailed list of such projects could be made. But there are good reasons for not lengthening the list here. It could not pretend in any event to be "complete" or "correct." An agenda asks questions. As most of us trained in the law believe, asking the right questions requires knowledge and understanding already sufficient to approach correct answers. We are not at that happy stage with respect to sentencing. What we know, mainly, is that the present state of affairs is grimly unsatisfactory. To repair it, we need the investment of substantial resources, high talent, and long, continuous attention. My main proposal, then, is that type of commitment. I turn to that final topic.

A COMMISSION ON SENTENCING

Using the jargon of our time, entirely apt in this instance, there are huge needs for organized research and development in the field of sentencing. As is true in other domains, the notion of research *and development* in this one must embrace more than the generation of scholarly studies, though such studies are surely wanted. There must be a commitment to change, to application of the learning as it is acquired. There must be recognition that the subject will never be definitively "closed," that the process is a continuous cycle of exploration and experimental change.

Since we deal with the law, the normal agency of change is, increasingly, the legislature. But the subject of sentencing is not steadily exhilarating to elected officials. There are no powerful lobbies of prisoners, jailers, or, indeed, judges, to goad and reward. Thus, accounting in good part for our plight, legislative action tends to be sporadic and impassioned, responding in haste to momentary crises, lapsing then into the accustomed state of inattention. It follows that an effective program of research and development should ideally modify in suitable fashion the existing procedure for implementing experiments through change.

These thoughts about the long pull lead to my proposed "Commission on Sentencing." The name is only a mode of brief description, tendered with neither pride of authorship nor authority. Even that disclaimer may come too late to restore the credit lost by the suggestion of still another commission. Risking that, I solicit your attention for only a while longer: this commission is meant to do much more than study and report, and it is tendered as the most important single suggestion in this book.

The proposed commission would be a permanent agency responsible for (1) the study of sentencing, corrections, and parole; (2) the formulation of laws and rules to which the studies pointed; and (3) *the actual enactment of rules,* subject to traditional checks by Congress and the courts. The third is emphasized, not because of a claim to novelty, but because it is thought to be especially important if the commission is to be an effective instrument of reform rather than a storage place.

To particularize a little, personnel is a good starting point. The commission would require prestige and credibility. It would be necessary to find for it people of stature, competence, devotion, and eloquence. The kinds of people—a matter, like others, only broached here for discussion—could include lawyers, judges, penologists, and criminologists. They should also include sociologists, psychologists, business people, artists, and, lastly for emphasis, former or present prison inmates. This final group sounded like a somewhat heady addition when this thought was first written, as part of a lecture, early in 1971. Since then, with prison riots and other events sweeping along in today's flood tides of change, it has become a familiar item. Prisoners have begun to appear in commissions of inquiry and similar bodies.* If by no means a novelty, the idea is a good one. The American Correctional Association, in August 1972, resolved to add "ex-offenders" to its board of directors. The similar proposal here does not envisage an approach to government of prisons by consent. It merely recognizes what took too long to become obvious—that the recipients of penal "treatment" must have relevant things to say about it.

In its capacity as a research organization, the commission would not attempt to supersede scholarly efforts already under way in universities and elsewhere. Instead, it would draw upon such enterprises, initiate new ones, and, in

* Our subject abounds in addenda and ironies. When I wrote the sentence on which this footnote hangs, I had prominently in mind the New York Commission headed by N.Y.U. Law School Dean Robert B. McKay which was studying the tragic conflict at the Attica prison in September 1971. That commission, which had not yet reported when the above was written, numbered an ex-convict in its membership. The commission's report, discussing the legal restrictions upon people who have served their sentences, contains this relevant passage:

> . . . the restrictions are so obscure that neither the judges who appointed this Commission nor the Governor who gave it life through an executive order nor the Commission itself realized that one of its members was legally ineligible to serve because he was an ex-convict—the very experience which commended him to the appointing judge.

Attica—The Official Report of the New York State Special Commission on Attica (New York, Bantam Books, 1972), p. 101.

addition, conduct studies of its own. Early in its career, the commission would inventory its domain, chart programs of inquiry, and set priorities. Subject always to ongoing revision, these initial measures would supply the framework for both the tapping of outside studies and the organization of projects within the agency.

In the nature of this proposal, the whole program might best be left in this abstract form. Despite the ring of certainty my rhetoric commonly shares with that of others in the legal profession, a major point of these polemics is meant to identify a large sea of ignorance in which we all find ourselves. If the commission here envisaged should be born, I would not wish or pretend to dictate its program. Hoping that is clear, I would merely offer for consideration one thought for a project that might follow from a basic defect (as I see it) in the sentencing process. I have dwelt at length upon both the lack of agreed factors to be considered and the lack of any agreed procedure for weighing or measuring such factors in determining the sentence. I have posited the possibility of a calculus or profile to explain and accompany each sentence. The study of this possible device strikes me as a challenging enterprise capable of engaging scholars for a long time. The enterprise would begin with a clearer definition than I have been able to give of the projected model. It would call at an early stage for extensive research and analysis to evolve acceptable tables of the material factors—or alternative lists to be proposed for policy decisions. A sophisticated program might well include experimental runs in selected courts—not because we are willing to risk men's fates as experimental subjects but because civilized tests of this kind could readily be controlled and corrected to ensure that those affected fared at least as well as they would have in the absence of such measures.

Leaving these musings as imaginary program director, I elaborate briefly the proposed interest of the commission in the enactment of changes its work would prompt. An agency of this character may serve legitimately as a kind of "lobby" built into the structure of government. The commission could, in this sense, represent those sentenced as well as those charged with custody and treatment. Agriculture, labor, business, investors, and others have long had their spokesmen or special guardians in the various departments and agencies. Lately, reflecting a variety of things we seem to care about as a nation, the consumer has been elbowing his way into the apparatus. Prisoners and jailers cannot be excluded much longer, unless we propose to deflect the course of our development in sharp and dubious ways.

Beyond its role as spokesman, the commission would have the function of actually enacting rules—i.e., making law. This suggestion would presumably generate controversy; legislators do not (and should not) lightly delegate their authority. Nevertheless, there is both precedent and good reason for delegating in this instance. As I have said, the subjects of sentencing, corrections, and parole are going to need ongoing study and an indefinite course of revision. Sweeping changes of policy, touching basic principles and institutions, will naturally remain for the legislature to determine from time to time. But relative details, numerous and cumulatively important, neither require nor are likely to receive from the legislature the necessary measure of steady attention. Thinking along such lines, Congress has delegated in a variety of fields—e.g., securities, transportation, communications—rulemaking powers with substantial day-to-day impact upon the affected areas. The suggestion here contemplates an analogous arrangement.

I have not tried, because I think it would not be useful, to formulate a precise division of lawmaking functions between Congress and the proposed commission. This would itself be a matter for study, debate, and, like the rest, improvements with experience. It would undoubtedly be reserved for Congress itself to determine the allowable purposes of sanctions, the basic kinds of treatment and punishment facilities, and the ranges of penalties for specific offenses. Merely as tentative and partial illustrations, it might be provided that the commission could prescribe in rules of general application the factors to be considered in individual sentences, the weight assignable to any specific factor, and details of sentencing and parole procedures.

Under our intricate system of checks and balances, the matters within the commission's province would be subject to a variety of "final" decisions by the several organs of government. Rules made by the commission within the scope of its authority would presumably be "binding" upon the courts as well as other agencies, though this might take some getting used to. At the same time, the courts would probably exercise their customary role of checking to see that the commission did not exceed its delegated authority under the law. On this, the scope and meaning of statute law, Congress would retain its usual last word in the form of the power to amend and repeal. And the whole—statutes and rules alike—would be limited by the Constitution, on which the judges in our system have the ultimate say. With this array of familiar safeguards, there would be no appreciable danger of desperately radical departures by the commission.

In any event, it is time to check the lawyer's appetite for procedural details * and move toward a conclusion. The uses of a commission, if one is created, will warrant volumes of debate and analysis. For this moment and this writer, the main thing is to plead for an instrumentality, whatever its name or detailed form, to marshal full-time wisdom and power against the ignorance and the barbarities that characterize sentencing for crimes today.

* But not to apologize for it. See footnote above, at page 59.

Concluding with a plea for action and a proposed form of action fairly reflects the basic ambition of this book. Though it is a revised version of lectures at a law school, and though my colleagues in the legal profession are warmly welcome readers, the hope is for a broader audience. I am not the first to paraphrase Clemenceau and say the law is too important to entrust to lawyers and judges. The great reforms of the law have always required the active exertions of an informed constituency broader than the legal profession. Lawyers and judges, tending to be human, are not likely to greet with rampant enthusiasm demands for change in their settled ways. (Indeed, our occupational habits have been thought intrinsically hostile to change, but I doubt that the recent history of the United States sustains that thought.) Moreover, even if we exhibited all the good will in the world, legal people would remain a small minority. We need from others every kind of support—moral, emotional, political—to pursue ends our training may lead us to perceive as good.

So to any reader who has come to this concluding paragraph—but perhaps somewhat especially to the lay reader—I would urge that you not close the topic along with the book. The topic has to do with monstrous evils perpetrated daily for all of us, and with our implicit or express acquiescence. The need for change is clear. Our justly proud awareness that "we the people" have the power should carry with it a corollary sense of duty. It is our duty to see that the force of the state, when it is brought to bear through the sentences of our courts, is exerted with the maximum we can muster of rational thought, humanity, and compassion.